BEHOLD!

The FEAR of the LORD

UNDERSTANDING THE GOODNESS AND SEVERITY OF GOD

STACI L. KITCHEN

Unless otherwise indicated, Bible quotations are taken from The Holy Bible, King James Version. Public Domain

Scriptures indicated AMP, NKJV, ESV, and NLT are from:

The Amplified Bible Copyright © 1954, 1958, 1962, 1964, 1987 by Zondervan Bible Publishers and the Lockman Foundation

The Holy Bible, New King James Version®. Copyright © 1982 by Thomas Nelson. Used by permission. All rights reserved.

The Holy Bible, English Standard Version. ESV® Text Edition: 2016. Copyright © 2001 by Crossway Bibles, a publishing ministry of Good News Publishers.

The Holy Bible, New Living Translation, copyright © 1996, 2004, 2015 by Tyndale House Foundation. Used by permission of Tyndale House Publishers, Inc., Carol Stream, Illinois 60188. All rights reserved.

For more information, email staci.lavaughn.kitchen12@gmail.com

ISBN: Paperback 979-8-218-05252-2,   eBook 979-8-218-28793-1

Editor and Interior Designer: Deborah A. Gaston, deborahgaston.com

Cover Designers: Samaria Kitchen, skitchen143@gmail.com

Alicia Redmond, www.aliciaredmond.com/bookcoversmatter

I dedicate this book to our children and future generations. May you grow continually in the knowledge and the reverential fear of the Lord.

Contents

Acknowledgments

I want to first thank Holy Spirit for the Spirit of the fear of the Lord.

I acknowledge my husband, Paul, for our 27-year marriage journey that has taught me to love like Christ, forbear, suffer long, and forgive. I appreciate all you do for our family.

I thank my daughter, Samaria. You took hold of the vision and allowed God to use your creative gifts to bring the cover to life.

I thank Apostle Valarie Randleman for being a supportive mentor in the infant stages of my writing. You were there when I first conceived of this book, so you are seeing it from heart to finish; Alicia Redmond, my friend, fellow scribe, and "focus and finish" accountability partner; the late Apostle Bernard Boulton, coach, and advisor, for his prophetic insight and encouragement in my scribal and creative endeavors.

My pastor, Apostle Brian Williams, thank you for teaching sound doctrine. It has enriched me immensely. Patricia Dawkins, my friend and prayer partner, thank you for your love, support, and prayers; Pastor Lisa Banks, your prayers, support, and counsel have been a lifeline—thank you!

And, Deborah Gaston, thank you for being a patient and steady midwife and helping me see the value of sharing my walk in the fear of the Lord. My story is coming!

Foreword

For every season we encounter, whether natural or spiritual, the rapidly changing landscape of our times may usher in or evoke fear. In these times, one may succumb to the tide of fear or awaken in the Spirit, look to the Lord for wisdom, and ultimately learn the fear of the Lord afresh. The fear of the Lord gives renewed strength, courage, and resolve to His sons and daughters to trust Him even more so in sundry times.

Staci Kitchen writes this book from personal experience—learning and gaining wisdom while understanding that the fear of the Lord gives us balance to love what He loves and hate what He hates. As you read this book from beginning to end, Staci carefully pens based on her life having lived in fear, exposing its triggers, and with fresh eyes and a steadfast heart, clearly articulating walking in the fear of the Lord. Let this labor of love challenge you to move beyond a head knowledge of the fear of the Lord to a heart ablaze again, awaiting the coming of our Lord.

Thank you, Staci, for writing this timely book!

Apostle Valarie L Randleman
Contributing Author, *Junia Arise Apostolic Women on the Frontlines*

Preface

I thought I was writing a book about fear. I was prepared, after many seasons of battling this spirit, to get free once and for all. I had participated in some powerful ministry lessons, sermons, and challenges, each providing a measure of deliverance, but I still felt the chains had not been completely broken. I sensed the Lord wanted me to write a book about it. Little did I know that this book was a journey inside a journey to understand the root of my fear.

See, fear manifests because of God. He is the First and Last, the Beginning and the End; if there is fear, it's because there is a God to be feared. One God, Almighty, with whom we all have to do— He is the One to be feared.

However, I started by drafting ideas that I believed were relevant to the fear I *thought* was going to be the focus of this book. As I began to go deeper in my writing, prayer, and study of the Word, I sensed God was leading me in a different direction. I was getting ready to do an entire exposé on the devil and his schemes to bring us into bondage through fear.

The Lord had another plan, and He led me to Proverbs 9:10, *"The fear of the Lord is the beginning of wisdom, and knowledge of the Holy is understanding."* It was like a light came on. I was not about to spend the next 12 or so chapters focusing on the devil. Sure, he has a hand in magnifying our fears and using them to deceive us out of our rightful place in God as sons. However, God revealed to me in the development of this book that it is about the fear of the Lord, not fear of the devil and what he can do. Until we have an understanding and revelation of that, we cannot understand fear.

Getting free of fear—the bad kind that the devil uses or that we simply walk in out of our sin nature—requires the fear of the Lord. When we fear God, we don't fear anything.

It's not that we are never afraid, but we are not led by the fear and foreboding that comes from our sin nature or the enemy.

The fear of the Lord is reverential. It is to be in awe of the holiness and purity of God, to be amazed at Him and to honor Him accordingly. This is where we see the other fear undone. Because we will recognize and have a true revelation of Who He Is. Everything else pales in comparison. The temptations to exalt anything else are diminished as we are ever conscious of His Ever-presence, and we are reminded that we act in full view of His watchful Eye.

That awareness causes us to pause and consider Him. So, we respond accordingly. The fear of the Lord is the beginning of wisdom and knowledge of the Holy is understanding. Once we acknowledge Him in His holiness, and we seek Him to know Him intimately, every other thing that gets in the way of honoring Him is quickly deemed an enemy. And rightly so. We would do well to truly seek the fear of the Lord—to know Him for ourselves and keep His holy commands ever before us. Not out of being afraid of Him but out of reverence for Him – because He is Holy. This brings confidence and is a shield against deception.

Sure, we are all prone but when we walk in the fear of the Lord we triumph over fear because the fear of the Lord brings with it wisdom and understanding. Deception has no power because our proximity to God causes us to see things differently. We have God's Wisdom and Understanding so we have the ability to recognize fear and deception and take authority over it. This is an awesome revelation that we can take to the bank.

I still get around to dealing with fear. However, it doesn't get center stage, although that may be the presenting issue for the reader. It was for me. But if we come to know God, fear must bow. It's that simple.

Now that we have a context, read this book with an open heart. Allow God to touch the places in you that you have not fully surrendered to Him. Examine the ways you may have allowed fear to gain an in roads because you have not truly entered into the fear of the Lord. When you turn the last page, my hope is that you take the next steps to go deeper in God and see fear undone in your own life. Because you truly will have the fear of the Lord.

Reflection: Laying Fear on the Altar

As I paused to consider my consecration offering to the Lord, I clearly heard that God desires obedience over sacrifice. So, I give Him the thing that has held me hostage and kept my obedience at bay—Fear! I desire to see The Lord infinitely greater than anything. Period.

When God speaks and gives me an instruction, I want to respond swiftly and completely. I don't need a "feeling" or some supernatural fuzzy sensation to move in obedience. I simply need the fear of the Lord. Instead, I had been fearing what man could do to me, allowing fear to cage me in, thinking it was protecting me when it was really a prison. I have had to repent of the error and ask God to give me the grace to simply obey and trust Him with the outcome, whatever it may be.

Truth is worth dying for and living a lie is no life at all. Yet I know as long as our Heavenly Father has a plan and purpose for our lives, He will preserve us. To live in fear is to live a lie, and I won't live a lie because I have the Spirit of Truth inside me. "Greater is He that is in me than he that is in the world" (1 John 4;4).

The answer is the Fear of the Lord. So, I lay ungodly fear on the altar and walk in the reverential fear of the Lord. Abiding in His Presence, discovering who I am in Him, and embracing the revelation of Who He is, trusting in Him. I enter into the knowledge of the fear of the Lord, and I walk soberly, no longer presuming to do things in the Name of the Lord, acting on His behalf or speaking for the Lord, yet having no reverence for Him because I don't truly know Him or His Nature.

I set my heart to seek The Lord diligently, to open my heart and allow Him to reveal Himself to me—that I would have the knowledge of God. In pursuing His Presence, my life would bear Godly fruit and glorify The Lord.

Introduction

I have written this book by the leading of Holy Spirit. It was born out of the revelation of my personal need to adjust and balance my understanding of the fear of the Lord. To be clear, the fear of the Lord is:

- **Reverence**
- **Awe**
- **Fear**
- **Terror (for those who willingly and unrepentantly sin)**
- **Honor**
- **Wonder**
- **Amazement**
- **Obedience**
- **Deference**
- **Respect**

By relinquishing our ways, we embrace holiness, righteousness, and truth through Jesus. It will cause us to praise, worship, bow down, cry, and repent. It will apprehend us and lead us into a deep love and respect for the Father.

God is holy and kind, but He is also just, righteous, and true. We must not simply see God as all anger and wrath, nor should we relegate His character to only grace and forbearance, but we must see His Divine character as the only One Whose nature is pure and holy that makes Him Who He Is. We don't dissect Him from all His divine qualities, but we must see Him in His manifold nature, simultaneously being Who He Is.

God simply Is.

And out of His Holy nature flows love, righteousness, justice, mercy, truth, and, yes, wrath. We want to see God as expressing only His love, but fail to see and accept that His hatred of sin and unrighteousness flows from His love.

Conversely, we can only see Him in His anger and wrath and miss the mercy, grace, and kindness flowing from His love. We must have a revelation of true love to give us corrective lenses. The truth is, God is love, and His zeal is expressed in His jealousy over us and His anger and righteous indignation over sin and injustice. He is good, and His kindness is expressed in His grace, mercy, patience, and forbearance. That He sent Jesus Christ, His only begotten Son, to redeem us is evidence of His goodness and love.

> *But God commendeth His love toward us, in that while we were yet sinners, Christ died for us (Romans 5:8).*

So why do we have such difficulty balancing our perspective of Who God Is and embracing all facets of His Holy nature? Until we have the corrective lens of Scripture, the Word of God, Holy Spirit's eyes to see, and an up-close and personal, intimate relationship and encounter with God, we will continue to have a skewed, perverted view of Him. We will make Him in our own image. So when we hear "the fear of the Lord," we either automatically think fear and terror, or we give space for admiration and amazement but not for His anger, righteous indignation, or wrath.

The fear of the Lord should not only inspire awe and amazement at His works but should apprehend us and call us to repentance and obedience. It should cause us to desire to please God and be faithful to His Word. We don't simply love and revere Him with our emotions but move in obedience because of Who He Is.

We must receive God, act according to Who He Is, and not make Him in our own image. When we only see a wonder-working God but not a God who judges, who gets angry or even grieved over sin, suffering, and injustice, we will only admire Him and not be compelled to worship Him in obedience.

To fear the Lord is to hate evil… (Proverbs 8:13a)

… by the fear of the Lord men depart from evil (Proverbs 16:6b).

Evidence of the fear of the Lord is not songs we sing to Him; it's not our prayers, fasting, alms-giving, etc. All those things have a place in honoring God. But if we don't hate evil and depart from it, we do not fear the Lord.

As we grow in the knowledge of God, He reveals Himself to us in the secret place of prayer, through our daily walk with Him and through the trials of life. As He reveals Himself more and more, we become established in the fear of the Lord and begin to live in honor, reverence, and obedience to Him. We love what He loves and hate what He hates. Our devotion is to Him, and our hearts will cling to His. It will even change our desires and constrain us from sin. God is not simply looking to be admired; He seeks our devotion and obedience. True worship of God flows not only out of acknowledging and praising Him but out of doing what He says.

In the chapters that follow, we will come to a greater revelation of the fear of the Lord and allow God to reveal more of His Holy Nature so that we embrace Him for Who He says He Is, knowing that He is good, and we don't have to be afraid of anything else.

Chapter 1

The Fear of the Lord is the Beginning of Wisdom

*The fear of the Lord is the beginning of wisdom:
and knowledge of the holy is understanding.*

Proverbs 9:10

*The reverent and worshipful fear of the Lord
is the beginning (the chief and choice part) of
wisdom, and the knowledge of the Holy One
is insight and understanding.*

Proverbs 9:10 AMPC

The fear of the Lord begins with God—acknowledging God and Who He Is. God reveals Himself through the Holy Scriptures of the Bible. This is His primary means of revelation of His Person, Character, Nature, Names, attributes, qualities, and all that makes Him the Supreme Being. He also reveals His heart, mind, plan, and purpose for mankind. In the Bible, we learn Who He Is.

It is not enough to know about God or to hear about Him. We can know Him not only by reading His Word but also by knowing Him experientially. This is His desire.

Most of us have come to know fear—the kind that brings apprehension, evil foreboding, and even terror. This was my life before I began my journey with God. I was afraid of any and everything. Afraid to live, afraid to die, afraid of failure, afraid of success, afraid of the devil, afraid of God – I was a walking basket case. Because I did not truly know God, I was just a fearful person. It wasn't always evident but I know the thoughts I harbored and the dread of life that consumed me daily from the time I was a young child, until well into adulthood.

This is not the fear that God would have us walk in. To fear God is to reverence Him. It is respect and honor considering His holiness, preeminence, and omnipotence. These qualities belong to God alone. The Scriptures describe God as Father, God of all creation, and Father of all.

> *But now, O Lord, thou art our father; we are the clay, and thou our Potter; and we are the work of thy hand (Isaiah 64:8).*
>
> *Like a father that pitieth his children, so the Lord pitieth them that fear him (Psalm 103:13).*
>
> *There is one body, and One Spirit, even as ye are called in one hope of your calling; one Lord, one faith, one baptism, one God and <u>Father of all,</u> who is above all and through all and in you all (Eph. 4:4-6 emphasis added).*

The Scriptures reveal God as the Word.

> *In the beginning was the Word and <u>the Word was with God</u> and the Word was God. The same was in the beginning with God. All things were made by him and without him was not anything made that was made (John 1:1-4 emphasis added).*

Nothing was made without God, and God created everything by His Word. The person of Jesus Christ is God's Word.

> *And the Word was made flesh, and dwelt among us, and we beheld his glory, the glory as of the only begotten of the Father, full of grace and truth (John 1:14).*

God is also revealed in Holy Spirit. Given by Jesus Christ that we may receive power, grace, and revelation of truth, Holy Spirit is the third Person of the Godhead.

> *Howbeit when he, the Spirit of truth is come, he will guide you into all truth; for he shall not speak of himself; but whatsoever he shall hear, that he shall speak; and he shall show you things to come (John 16:13).*

As we walk with God, we grow in our knowledge of Who He is and engage with and encounter Jesus Christ and Holy Spirit. Jesus reconciled us to God, and Holy Spirit guides us throughout our journey with God testifying of Him.

God as Our Father

One of our greatest challenges in walking in the fear of the Lord is reconciling Him as the All-powerful God and His nature as Father. Negative experiences with earthly fathers have made it difficult to see God as Father, much less a good Father. The nature of the Father is to love, care, provide for, protect, and cover His children.

Though I have enjoyed a positive relationship with my natural father most of my life, my parents' separation and subsequent divorce left me with wounds and fears of loss and abandonment, although my father was very present in my life. I came to realize that once I began to seek God and desire to get to know Him, I had projected my fears and father wounds on God, and wrestled many years to trust Him and His Word. I had an ungodly fear of God that was based on my experience with my father. Like many who have grown up in broken homes, the pain and hurt of my father not being in the home, left me feeling abandoned when my parents broke up. So, much of my walk with the Lord has been reconciling my experience with my natural father and the reality of Who God Is. Once God gave me corrective lenses through which to view His Holy Nature as Father, I was able to begin to embrace Him as a good Father.

7

Our earthly fathers are to represent God the Father in nature and their role in our lives. Sadly, because of sin, the role of a father has been perverted; the family structures through which men are to gain their identities as children of God have been destroyed, leaving broken and dysfunctional homes where fathers were either absent, abused, or traumatized. This cycle has devastated sons and daughters to the extent that it has colored our perception of God. God is not like man; He is good, and He is a good Father. Once we open our hearts to see that, like a loving father, He instructs, protects, and corrects, we are able to receive Him as Father—our heavenly Father. We often come to revere our earthly fathers but can still neglect to honor and reverence God based on our experience with our natural fathers.

If we have experienced hardship because of lack, it is easy to doubt that God will provide. If we have experienced abandonment, we will not believe God is always with us. The truth is, no matter what we have gone through, it does not change God's nature as Father. If we allow Him to reveal Himself as Father and us as His sons and daughters, we will enjoy the benefits of that relationship.

The Names and Nature of God

God is revealed by His many Names. His Names give us a further understanding of Who He Is and should lead us to reverence Him. His Nature is not limited to the Names we know, as He is infinite in His nature and ability.

In Hebrew, the covenant name for God is Yahweh. When Yahweh (God) revealed Himself to Israel through Moses, He revealed Himself this way:

> *... this is my name forever and this is my memorial to all generations (Genesis 3:15).*

God revealed Himself as Yahweh—their God—and invited them into covenant with Him that would take them on what was supposed to be a three-day journey out to the wilderness after he used Moses to deliver them from the bondage of

Egypt. Yahweh knew that they were not prepared to meet with the enemy nations they would encounter on their way to the Promised Land. He took them the long way around the mountainous desert so that the battles of their enemies would not cause them to turn back to Egypt.

God was their God, and He revealed Himself as a covenant God Who would protect His people. He would ensure that they made it to the Promised Land. There, they were to worship Him by offering Him a sacrifice. In return, Yahweh promised to deal with their Egyptian captors. He made a covenant with them to be their God and their Deliverer, and true to His Name and Nature, He kept His promise.

The Lord's Name is powerful. It elicits fear when spoken, invoked, or declared. Nations came to fear Israel when they realized God was on her side. God revealed Himself as:

- **Almighty God (Genesis 17:1,2)**
- **The Most High God (Genesis 14:18-22)**
- **Yahweh Jireh—The Lord will Provide (Genesis 22:14)**
- **Yahweh-Sabaoth—The Lord of Hosts/the Lord Almighty (1 Samuel 1:3)**
- **Yahweh Makkedesh—The Lord Who Sanctifies (Leviticus 20:7, 8)**

He has also been referred to as:

- **Father**
- **I Am**
- **Rock**
- **King of Glory**
- **Holy**
- **Deliverer**
- **Defender**
- **Strong Tower**

His Names are as infinite as His Nature. The key to the revelation of God is in relationship and fellowship with Him. We grow in the knowledge of God by spending time with Him, seeking Him in prayer, and studying His Word. When we accept His Son, Jesus Christ, we have direct access to God the Father, enabling us to embark upon a journey of discovering Who God Is.

Chapter 2

God's Holy Spirit

Howbeit when he, the Spirit of truth, is come,
he will guide you into all truth: for he shall
not speak of himself: but whatsoever he shall
hear, that he shall speak: and he shall shew
you things to come.

John 16:13

Jesus Christ gives Holy Spirit so that we may receive revelation of the Truth. Holy Spirit is the third person of the Godhead and is revealed in Scripture as:

- **Comforter (John 14:16)**
- **Spirit of Truth (John 14:17)**
- **The Holy Ghost (1 Corinthians 6:19-20)**
- **The Spirit of Grace (Hebrews 10:29)**

Holy Spirit is a Person. He

- Speaks
- Guides
- Reveals
- Shows
- Reproves
- Teaches
- Leads
- Convicts
- Endows
- Anoints
- Indwells
- Breathes

Holy Spirit is given by Jesus Christ to those who believe to empower them to live holy and set apart for God. He abides in and walks beside us. We need Holy Spirit to receive revelation, grace, and power. Holy Spirit dwells in us. The Bible tells us that our bodies are the temple of the Holy Spirit (I Corinthians 6:19).

Holy Spirit also works in us to do the will of God, revealing God's will and giving us knowledge and understanding of the Wisdom of God (Philippians 2:13).

Holy Spirit also convicts us:

> *And when he is come, he will reprove the world of sin, and of righteousness, and of judgment (John 16:8).*

Because He is the Spirit of Truth, He holds the measuring stick by which we will all be judged. When He convicts, we become keenly aware of our condition before Him.

We cannot talk about God without talking about Holy Spirit and Jesus. Understanding that God manifests in All Three—Father, Son, and Holy Spirit—is critical. Because He works in us, we can respond according to His promptings in our spirit and conscience.

We can:

- Quench the Spirit by ignoring His promptings or repeatedly dismissing his leading
- Blaspheme the Spirit by demonstrating a gross form of irreverence where we attribute the work of Holy Spirit to evil or the evil one. (This comes from a heart that is hardened to the Truth. Once that occurs, there is no repentance or forgiveness as the thing needed to produce it is lacking)
- Grieve the Spirit by engaging in conduct that is unbecoming of a child of God

Holy Spirit is our Comforter. He walks alongside us to help us through life. The Greek word for Comforter is *parakletos.* It means intercessor, counselor, advocate, comforter, or one who pleads the cause of another, bestowing spiritual aid and consolation. We need Holy Spirit. He is the very Breath of God, possessing the Mind and Intelligence of God, His power, and His Agency.

Those who belong to God receive the Holy Spirit. We can also be baptized in the Holy Spirit and endued with power, allowing us to walk in the fruit and gifts of the Spirit. The Fruit of the Spirit manifests as we surrender to Christ and grow in intimacy with God. The Gifts of the Spirit are given and demonstrate God's power at work in a person's life. Ideally, we would operate in the fruit of the Spirit and the Gifts of the Spirit.

The Fruit of the Spirit

> *But the Fruit of the Spirit is love, joy, peace, longsuffering, gentleness, goodness, faith, meekness, temperance, against such there is no law (Galatians 5:22-23).*

The Fruit of the Holy Spirit is not just ordinary "fruit." It is the character that is developed in those who submit to God to be transformed and formed in Christ's image, the image of the Father.

- **Love:** *"Charity suffereth long, and is kind: charity envieth not; charity vaunteth not itself, is not puffed up, doth not behave itself unseemly, seeketh not her own, is not easily provoked, thinketh no evil; rejoiceth not in iniquity, but rejoiceth in the truth; beareth all things, believeth all things, hopeth all things, endureth all things. Charity (love) never fails..." (1 Corinthians 13:4-7, 8a)*
- **Joy:** *"But godliness with contentment is great gain" (1 Timothy 6:6); "For the kingdom of God is not meat and drink; but righteousness, and peace, and joy in the Holy Ghost" (Romans 14:17)*
- **Peace:** *"And the peace of God, which passeth all understanding, shall keep your hearts and minds through Christ Jesus" (Philippians 4:7).*
- **Longsuffering:** *"And not only so, but we glory in*

tribulations also: knowing that tribulation worketh patience; and patience, experience; and experience, hope" (Romans 5: 3-4).

- **Gentleness:** *"Pleasant words are as an honeycomb, sweet to the soul, and health to the bones" (Proverbs 16:24).*
- **Goodness:** *"As we have therefore opportunity, let us do good unto all men, especially unto them who are of the household of faith" (Galatians 6:10).*
- **Faith:** *"Now faith is the substance of things hoped for, the evidence of things not seen. For by it the elders obtained a good report. Through faith we understand that the worlds were framed by the word of God, so that things which are seen were not made of things which do appear" (Hebrews 11: 1- 3).*
- **Meekness:** *"Put on therefore, as the elect of God, holy and beloved, bowels of mercies, kindness, humbleness of mind, meekness, longsuffering, forbearing one another and forgiving one another" (Colossians 3:12).*
- **Temperance:** *"And every man that striveth for mastery is temperate in all things. (1 Corinthians 9: 25). (The grace for self-control, discipline, and moderation is a fruit of the Spirit).*

Holy Spirit is represented by:
- **Fire**
- **Water**
- **Power**
- **Wisdom**
- **Truth**
- **Grace**

He IS the Spirit of Truth, so He reveals the mind of God and is the Wisdom of God.

> *Howbeit when he, the Spirit of Truth, is come, he will guide you into all truth: for he shall not speak of himself; but whatsoever he shall*

hear, that he shall speak; and he shall show you
things to come (John 16:13).

Holy Spirit leads and guides us into revelations of truth. This revelation comes as a knowing, that may not be accompanied by what can be seen or known by the five senses. For instance, when you read the Bible, a word, phrase, Scripture, story, or picture stands out, jumps out, or comes alive. Holy Spirit may point you to a passage or series of scriptures, words, or events to reveal truth. He will never contradict His Word, and what He reveals will always be consistent in spirit, principle, and intent of His Word and His Nature.

Holy Spirit will never lead you to do, say, or "reveal" something that goes against His Word. He will not violate His Word nor His holiness. He IS His Word; He is integral, meaning He is whole and complete in and of Himself; He and His Word are One. He is immutable and incorruptible. If you ever believe you are hearing from Holy Spirit, test it against the Word of God as revealed in the Bible. Holy Spirit will lead you into truth.

Beloved, believe not every spirit, but try the
spirits whether they are of God: because many
false prophets are gone out into the world (1
John 4:1).

Holy Spirit will always point to Jesus, Who is the Word. God magnifies His Word higher than His Name (Psalm 138:2). His Name sums up His Word. The infinite sum total of His Word makes Him Who He Is. When we truly fear the Lord, we acknowledge and seek Him, and wisdom and understanding come through His Word. His Word is Jesus, who is revealed through Scripture. Reading, studying, meditating, and praying through Scripture are vital to our faith and our very lives.

The best way to get to know God is through His Word and by devoting oneself to prayer and time in His Presence. The more time we spend in His Presence and prayer, the more we know Him. We learn of Him, and He reveals Himself more and more. When we spend time in God's Presence and get to know Him, His holiness is revealed, and we come to reverence Him. The more we spend time with Him, the more we see how awesome He Is, and we become more aware of our sin nature and our need for sanctification.

> *Who is a wise man and endued with knowledge among you? Let him shew out of a good conversation (actions, how he conducts himself) his works with meekness of wisdom. But if you have bitter envying and strife in your hearts, glory not and lie not against the truth. This wisdom descendeth not from above but is earthly, sensual, devilish. For where envying and strife is there is confusion and every evil work. But the wisdom that is from above is first pure, then peaceable, gentle, and easy to be entreated, full of mercy and good fruits, without partiality and without hypocrisy (James 3:13-17).*

The Scripture reveals His Wisdom as it is reflected in His Nature. Those who fear Him and have His Spirit will also show His nature.

> *But the fruit of the Spirit is love, joy, peace, longsuffering, gentleness, goodness, faith, meekness, temperance, against such there is no law (Galatians 5: 22-23).*

When we truly fear the Lord, we honor Him, trust Him, revere Him, and open our hearts to His will and plan for our lives. We respect that He is Sovereign, Holy, all-knowing, all-powerful, and superior in all things. We also acknowledge our need for His love, guidance, lordship, Wisdom, protection, and provision for our existence. The fear of the Lord is the beginning of wisdom. It is the starting point to revelation and understanding Who He Is and Who we are in Him, why we were created, and His perfect plan for us.

Revelation of the Manifold Spirit of God

And there shall come forth a rod out of the stem of Jesse, and a Branch shall grow out of his roots: and the spirit of the Lord shall rest upon him, the spirit of wisdom and understanding, the spirit of counsel and might, the spirit of knowledge and of the fear of the Lord; And shall make him of quick understanding in the fear of the Lord; and he shall not judge after the sight of his eyes neither reprove after the hearing of his ears (Isaiah 11: 1- 3).

These verses are a prophetic declaration of the coming of the Messiah, Jesus, revealing the Spirit of God that would and does rest upon Him. The Spirit of the Lord is described as wisdom, understanding, counsel, might, knowledge, and the fear of the Lord. These attributes reveal the manifold Spirit of God and the multifaceted nature of the operation of His Spirit that would rest upon Jesus.

Behold, my servant, whom I uphold; mine elect in whom my soul delighteth; I have put my spirit upon him: he shall bring forth judgment to the Gentiles (Isaiah 42:1).

The Spirit of the Lord is upon me: because the Lord hath anointed me to preach good tidings unto the meek; he hath sent me to bind up the brokenhearted, to proclaim liberty to the captives, the opening of the prison to them that are bound (Isaiah 61:1).

These scriptures prophesy the coming and ministry of Jesus through the Spirit of the Lord. God's nature is such that His Spirit is multi-dimensional, and His power is revealed in all

His dimensions. Though we will never be able to grasp all of His qualities and Who He is, what the Bible reveals of Him through Jesus Christ enables us to receive and recognize His power, wisdom, and righteousness at work in the earth. What a magnificent wonder that Jesus, who is God Himself, walked in the spirit of the fear of the Lord! This is evidence that He truly is the Source of all spiritual endowment. The ability to walk in the reverential fear of the Lord comes from the Spirit of God, giving us wisdom and understanding that we would "see" God spiritually, acknowledge Him, and be struck with wonder and amazement.

In the Old Testament, the Spirit of the Lord came upon and rested on the prophets to speak God's Word to His people. Certain individuals were filled with the Spirit of God, such as Bezaleel. Exodus 35:30 tells us that the Lord filled him with the Spirit of God in wisdom and understanding, knowledge, and all manner of workmanship. Not only was Bezaleel an artisan and craftsman who worked on the Temple, but he was also a teacher.

> *And I will give them one heart, and I will put a new spirit within you and I will take the stony heart out of their flesh; and will give them an heart of flesh, That they may walk in my statutes, and keep mine ordinances, and do them: and they shall be my people and I will be their God (Ezekiel 11:19–20).*

This prophecy in Ezekiel foretells God's plan to give His people a "new spirit," enabling them to walk in His statutes. Without the Spirit of the Lord, we will not have the wisdom or power to walk in righteousness. Both are needed and come only by the Spirit of the Lord.

The Presence of God

It is not unusual to hear *"the Lord is here," "God is in the room,"* or *"His presence is here."* This declaration commonly occurs in corporate settings, prayer, or even when a powerful

Word goes forth. Some may be in tune and keenly aware of His Presence, while others may not. Because God is eternal, He is ever-present. Because He is Spirit, His Presence must be discerned spiritually. The Presence of God may come in many manifestations, and the Scriptures give us language and metaphors.

- **A mighty rushing wind**
- **Fire**
- **Still small voice**
- **Cloud**
- **Rushing waters**

Some believe that God's Presence only manifests in dramatic ways. But upon seeking Him, anyone can come to know His Presence and when you've encountered Him. His Presence may be tangible as a sense of something weighty and glorious hovering over a worship service, and sweet smells and peace may accompany it. Or it may be as simple as a tickle of joy that arises in you for no apparent reason.

But how do we know when we have encountered or come into God's Presence? Do our emotions tell us that we are in His Presence? Is it a song that brings us to tears? Are the tears themselves evidence? If I don't "feel" Him, does that mean He is not present? Can we call Him to "come," or will He just show up? Is He always present with us, or must we call Him? These are all questions we may have as we seek to experience God in real-time. The awesome thing is we can.

Very early on in my walk with the Lord, I began to seek Him in earnest. I would learn for myself exactly what it meant to "feel" His Presence. It is not unusual for me to steal away to just seek the Lord and sit in His Presence. I might begin to sing a song to Him, pray, or just admire creation around me. Even just washing dishes and gazing out of the window, I'd have a tangible sense of peace and joy come upon me—this is His Presence.

Sometimes, it is hard to describe, and other times, it really comes like a rush of wind, and my whole countenance would change, and I knew I had been touched by God. Time would seem to stand still, and what seems like forever may be just moments, or I would lose sense of time because I would be captivated. It has been in these times that the Lord would reveal Himself in His manifold wisdom, goodness, righteousness, and all that He Is. It would never cease to amaze me. I knew I had encountered God because my heart had changed, and I knew it.

> *Christ dwells in your heart by faith (Ephesians 3:17).*

This promise is ours at salvation; true conversion will reveal it. By faith, we know Christ is always with us because He lives in our hearts.

> *For where two or three are gathered together in my name, there am I in the midst of them (Matthew 18:20).*

If two or more come together in His name, He says He is there. We can trust that He is in the midst when we come together for prayer, worship, and even fellowship on account of Him.

> *...I will never leave nor forsake thee (Hebrews 13:5).*

God has promised to be with us always.

> *And he said, My presence shall go with thee, and I will give the rest (Exodus 33:14).*

God's Presence is everything when we are walking through life. Knowing He is there and sees everything we face gives us a sense of abiding peace. His Presence is simply where He is and abides. We can enter His Presence through prayer, seeking Him in earnest, or responding to His call to His Presence.

> *"Deep calleth unto deep at the noise of thy water-spouts: All thy waves and thy billows are gone over me" (Psalm 42:7).*

You may experience a strong sense of God's beckoning to you to come into His Presence. In those times, He may come as a canopy over you as you pray, a tabernacle or place to worship, a secret place where you and God are intimate, a hiding place or shelter where you are safe and out of reach of the enemy.

The enemy cannot come into the Presence of God without being exposed. It's like the old process for developing photographs; once the light hits the film, it's exposed, and the picture is ruined.

> *"Thou wilt shew me the path of life: In thy Presence is fulness of joy; At thy right hand there are pleasures for evermore" (Psalm 16:11).*

Here is one of the ways you can discern the Lord's Presence—joy. Joy is not merely happiness but a supernatural state of being in God that does not change with circumstances. It is a confident sense of well-being and peace that abides within no matter what else is going on because of the Presence of God in us. It does not mean that we don't get sad or have other emotions, but joy remains in the midst of them.

> *"... for the joy of the Lord is your strength" (Nehemiah 8:10c).*

The presence of the Lord brings joy, and it strengthens us to face life and its challenges. A person with no joy has no strength to stand, but the one who abides in God has His presence, and joy is their portion. They are able to withstand adversities.

When the Spirit of the Lord is present, those who are indeed His and recognize His Presence:

- **Worship:** Expressing God's holiness and worthiness, exalting His Name in songs, praises, or movement
- **Adoration:** Giving thanks, telling God you love Him, pouring out words of expression
- **Fear:** Reverencing God, sometimes with silence, apprehension, listening, waiting

When Holy Spirit is present, we can expect:
- **Revelation/Prophecy:** God speaks a word in real-time, giving those present hope, strength, encouragement, direction, and even correction.
- **Miracles:** The power of God is manifest in miracles, signs and wonders, deliverance, and healing.
- **Songs:** The Presence of the Lord evokes songs that are messages directly from Him or to Him that reveal His heart.
- **Instruments:** Chords, keys, and sounds are played spontaneously, creating an atmosphere for what God wants to do among a people.
- **Repentance:** The Lord's Presence reveals the conditions of our hearts and can bring repentance, contrition, godly sorrow, and desire to change.
- **Transformation:** We are changed the more we abide in the Presence of the Lord because through intimacy with Him, the old man dies, and the new man comes forth

Prayer:
Lord, help me to acknowledge You as God above all things. Give me a revelation of Your manifold nature, wisdom, and understanding that only comes from You. I surrender my preconceived thoughts, thought patterns, and beliefs I have received about You that are not based in Truth, and I lean in to embrace Who You reveal You Are through Your Word and by Your Spirit. (Isaiah 33:6)

Chapter 3

The Knowledge of God

"But without faith, it is impossible to please him (God): for he that cometh to God must believe that He is, and that He is a rewarder of them that diligently seek Him

Hebrews 11:6

To know God requires a revelation of Who He Is. It is not simply to know about Him or believe that He exists "out there somewhere." The knowledge of God that leads to the fear of the Lord is acknowledging Him and honoring Him as He has revealed Himself. This comes through relationship, fellowship, and communion with Him.

In my walk with the Lord, I was saved and attended church, but it took me many years to even begin to get to know God. And because I didn't really know Him, I did not fear Him. Or rather, I did not reverence Him. I was learning about Him and being faithful to man in what I believed was honor to God, but I just didn't know Him. It took the Lord's chastening and correction for me to finally submit to learn the fear of the Lord. I thought I feared Him because I was afraid of Him, but it was not out of knowing Him. And I did much in His name without an intimate knowledge of Him. I would soon learn that doing things for God and believing in God did not mean I knew Him. But all of that would change.

The word "know" has a few connotations, one being intimate knowledge. When a man was said to "know" a woman, it was generally describing being sexual or intimate with her. The intimacy with which we come to know God is spiritual. It is an up close and intimate transparency type of knowing we seek—one where we are naked before God

23

and unashamed. Once I was able to just be honest with God and remove the fig leaves and coverings that I somehow believed would keep God from seeing who I really was, I came to know that He loved me and accepted me despite my faults, shortcomings, and waywardness.

The awesome thing is that the closer I got to God, the more I was able to rest in Him, and the desire to please Him with my life became more evident. I didn't feel ashamed but submitted to the conviction I felt when He would reveal things in my heart or my life that were not in alignment with His Word or His Divine plan for me. The Lord revealing His goodness to me allowed me to rest in Him and trust Him. Seeking Him diligently to know Him experientially has established me in the fear of the Lord, where I reverence Him from a place of love and honor.

When we recognize Him and have a revelation of Who He Is, we will seek to know Him, worship Him, praise Him, and thank Him for Who He Is. We become grateful for Him creating and giving us life and will seek Him for His plan for our lives. Acknowledging Him is to know and act like He exists and allow His Truth to open our hearts to receive more and more revelation from Him. When we have the reverential fear of the Lord, we bestow honor and respect on Him and respond to Who He Is with our worship, faith, trust, and obedience.

God has revealed Himself to us through His creation and as His creation.

> *For the wrath of God is revealed from heaven against all ungodliness and unrighteousness of men, who hold the truth in unrighteousness, <u>because that which may be known of God is manifest in them</u>, for God hath shewed it unto them. For the invisible things of him from the creation of the world are clearly seen, being understood by the things that are made, even his eternal power and Godhead; so that they are without excuse; because that, when they knew*

God, they glorified him not as God neither were thankful; but became vain in their imaginations, and their foolish heart was darkened (Romans 1:18-21 emphasis added).

God revealed to us that He Is. How do we know? Because this is His Word, and His Word is True. Deep inside us is the revelation of God and His holiness and righteousness. We have no excuse.

The fear of the Lord is the beginning of wisdom, and the knowledge of the Holy One is understanding (Proverbs 9:10 NKJV).

Because He is infinite in His Wisdom, first acknowledging Him is where we begin to understand Who He Is, His plan and purpose for creation, and our lives. The knowledge of God is the experiential knowledge of Him gained in communion with Him.

Hear the word of the Lord, ye children of Israel; for the Lord hath a controversy with the inhabitants of the land, because there is no truth, no mercy, nor knowledge of God (fear, reverence, acknowledgment of God) in the land, By swearing and lying and killing and stealing and committing adultery, they break out and blood toucheth blood (Hosea 4:1-2).

In Hosea, the Lord had an issue with the children of Israel, so He sent the prophet Hosea to give them a word of rebuke, correction, and judgment. They were committing all sorts of evil, sins, and injustices and acting as if they had no God to answer to—as if they did not know Him. He said there was "no knowledge of God in the land."

Surely, they knew God; they knew He existed. But their

actions showed that they did not fear Him. If they truly feared the Lord, they would not be so wanton in their wicked pursuits, lying, stealing, killing, and doing other things that violated the laws of God. Instead, they would conduct themselves as if they had to give an account to Him for their actions. This was not so with the children of Israel, and God expressed His displeasure and issued His divine judgment.

> *My people are destroyed for lack of knowledge: because thou hast rejected knowledge, I will also reject thee, that thou shalt be no priest to me, seeing thou hast forgotten the law of thy God, I will also forget thy children (Hosea 4:6).*

In other words, God was saying, "Because you have refused to acknowledge Me, you will face destruction. And because you have rejected Me, I will reject your children. The covenant privileges and rights you had will not be bestowed on your children because you failed to acknowledge Me."

The rebuke came because the children of Israel were engaged in ungodly behavior, forsaking God's Covenant to be a righteous people and practicing idolatry (Spiritual Adultery). They began to consult with idols and give over worship to them instead of God, Who delivered them, provided for them, and was covenanted to them. They turned away from God. They knew God but were not acknowledging Him as God, much less their God. Their lack of acknowledgment led to their destruction. God's standard for keeping covenant is first to fear Him, and then you will have understanding and knowledge of God. This is what keeps us sober and restrains us from sin.

Hosea 4:6 is often read as an admonishment about knowledge. But it is not only or all about what we know intellectually but Who we know experientially that preserves and keeps us from destruction. We must not replace our reverence for the Lord, our worship, honor, and acknowledgment of Him as God with trust in our own understanding and relying on our carnal knowledge. We must know God to have that reverential fear of Him.

> *Trust in the Lord with all thine heart; Lean not unto thine own understanding but in all thy ways acknowledge Him and he shall direct thy paths. Be not wise in thine own eyes: Fear the Lord, and depart from evil (Proverbs 3:5-7).*

> *For your obedience is come abroad unto all men. I am glad therefore on your behalf: but yet I would have you wise unto that which is good and simple concerning evil (Romans 16:19).*

The practical approach to the knowledge of God is to open your heart and seek His face. Go to God in prayer and ask Him to reveal Who He Is to you. When you genuinely desire to know Him, He will begin to reveal Himself. His primary way of doing this is through His Word. God seeks an intimate relationship with His creation. The word "know" connotes intimacy often associated with intercourse. God desires spiritual intercourse with us. This is holy and beautiful because it produces the fruit of the Spirit in us. It is intimacy with God in the secret place—the secret place is His Presence.

God desires us to be wise in what is good and simple concerning evil. To be simple is to be unsophisticated, naive, inexperienced with evil. For many of us, we have become too familiar and have too intimate a knowledge of evil, having practiced and experienced evil ourselves.

Coming into the revelation of God, He reveals His:

- **Preeminence:** Preeminence denotes superiority over all things

> *And He is the head of the body, the Church; who is the beginning, the firstborn from the dead;*

that in all things he might have preeminence (Colossians 1:18).

- **Holiness:** Holiness is the defining characteristic of God that is reserved for Him alone. It denotes pure goodness, righteousness, and truth unmatched by any other being, incorruptible and void of contamination.

  Exalt the Lord our God, and worship at His holy hill; For the Lord our God is holy (Psalm 99:9a).

  To whom then will ye liken me, or shall I be equal? Saith the Holy One (Isaiah 40:25).

- **Omniscience:** The word omniscient means infinite awareness, understanding, and insight, possessing complete and total universal knowledge and wisdom. God is All-knowing. He sees all, knows all, and knows the end from the beginning.

  Neither is there any creature that is not manifest in His sight, but all things are naked and open unto the eyes of Him with Whom we have to do (Hebrews 4:13).

  Remember the former things of old; for I am God and there is none else; I am God, and there is none like me, declaring the end from the beginning, and from ancient times, the things that are not yet done, saying, My counsel shall stand, and I will do my pleasure (Isaiah 46:9-10).

- **Omnipresence:** God is eternal and exists outside of time. Just as He sees all and knows all, all the time, at the same time, He is eternally existent—having no creator, no beginning, and no end. He is expressed through Jesus as His Word, described as the same yesterday, today, and forever. God is His Word, and His Word abides forever. He is immutable, and there is no shadow of turning with Him. The essence of Who He is does not change.

I beheld till the thrones were cast down, and the Ancient of Days did sit, whose garment was white as snow, and the hair of his head like pure wool: his throne was like the fiery flame, and his wheels as burning fire (Daniel 7:9).

I am Alpha and Omega, the beginning and the ending. Saith the Lord, which is, and which was, and which is to come, the Almighty (Revelation 1:8).

- **Sovereignty:** God is God Alone; He reserves the right and prerogative to choose any course of action and, in doing so, still maintains His holiness. When God does a thing, he consults with Himself. Because He is Creator of all, He rules and reigns supreme, far above all other created order and beings.

But our God is in the heavens; he hath done whatsoever he hath pleased (Psalm 115: 3).

- **Justice and Righteousness:** God is THE Supreme Ruler who rules in righteousness. Because He is Holy, pure, and True, so are His judgments. He does not rule unfairly, and He only judges justly. His Omniscience qualifies Him to judge matters righteously, and His character and nature ensure that His determinations are always right and righteous. He is not biased nor a respecter of persons. He can't be manipulated, corrupted, or tempted to pervert justice.

As Holy Creator, He alone establishes the standards and measures of truth and righteousness. Those measures are personified in Jesus Christ, Who is the Word made flesh. He embodied the standard of righteousness. When He judges, He judges by Himself. Judgment and Justice reside with Him and Him alone. He is justice. He and His Word are the same, and His Word is embodied in His Name.

> *Clouds and darkness are around about him: righteousness and judgment are the habitation of his throne (Psalm 97:2).*

- **Goodness:** God is good. All that He does is good. Even in His judgment, He acts out of His pure and Holy nature, which is good. God is not evil, and there is no evil in Him.

> *O give thanks unto the Lord, for He is good, for His mercy endureth forever (Psalm 136:1).*

- **Love:** God's loving nature is pure and unchanging affection toward His creation that desires the best for us and does all for our wellbeing. His love is unmatched and is not like man's. Out of His loving nature, He judges evil and protects His people.

> *Beloved, let us love one another: for love is of God; and everyone that loveth is born of God, and knoweth God. He that loveth not knoweth not God; for God is love (1 John 4: 7-8).*

Prayer:

Lord God, I desire intimate knowledge of You based on time spent in Your Presence. Father, ignite a fire within me that desires to seek You continually so that I may know You. (Proverbs 2:1-9; Psalm 25:14)

Chapter 4

How Fear Entered In

And the Lord called unto Adam, and said unto him, where art thou? And he said, I heard thy voice in the garden, and I was afraid because I was naked, and I hid myself.

Genesis 3:9-10

When we think of "fearing" God, we often associate it with negative feelings that someone or something will harm us. *The Oxford Dictionary* defines fear as "an unpleasant emotion caused by the belief that someone or something is dangerous, likely to cause pain or a threat."

It's no wonder even the thought of fearing God would cause apprehension. God did not create us to have this kind of fear, so where did it come from?

God created man in His image and in His likeness. He determined it was not good for man to be alone, so He caused a deep sleep to come upon Adam and formed Eve (woman) from Adam's rib. She would be called "woman" because she was taken from man and had a womb. The plan was that man would leave his mother and father and cleave to his wife, and they would become one flesh.

> *And they were both naked, the man and his wife, and were not ashamed (Genesis 2:25).*

When God created man and woman, Adam and Eve, He gave them dominion and charged them to be fruitful and multiply. God placed them in the Garden of Eden, and the earth yielded its increase. This was all by God's Divine providence. They enjoyed fellowship with God continually and walked with God in the cool of the day. God gave them access to every tree in the Garden, except for the tree of the knowledge of good and evil.

God is infinite in wisdom and power; He created all things and upholds all things by the Word of His power (Hebrews 1:3). His power and creative ability are immeasurable, boundless, and infinite. Imagine what it meant for Adam and Eve to have access to all of what God made available to them in the Garden!

Can you imagine the expanse of the Garden of Eden and that God had allowed them to eat from every tree except one? They could have eaten from every other tree and never come to the end of the Garden. The fruit and God's provision would continuously be available, and they would only have to tend to and dress the Garden.

There was one exception: God told Man he could eat of every tree except the Tree of the Knowledge of Good and Evil.

> *And the Lord God commanded the man, saying, of every tree of the garden thou mayest freely eat; But of the tree of the knowledge of good and evil thou shalt not eat of it: for in the day that thou eatest thereof thou shalt surely die (Genesis 2:16-17).*

Then along came the serpent.

> *Now the serpent was more subtil than any beast of the field which the Lord God had made. And he said unto the woman, Yea, hath God said, Ye shall not eat of every tree of the garden? (Genesis 3:1)*

The next few verses recount the woman attempting to respond to the serpent. She said, "God told us not to eat of the tree in the midst of the Garden nor touch it, or we would die."

The serpent lied to her by refuting God's Word. He then insinuated and accused God of withholding something from her, twisting God's instructions as if what He was withholding was somehow a threat to God, causing her to question God's motives and Character. The serpent revealed his true nature to accuse, twist, and deceive. When the woman told the serpent what God said, he responded that she "shall not surely die."

> *And the serpent said unto the woman, Ye shall not surely die. For God doth know that in the day ye eat thereof, then your eyes shall be opened, and ye shall be as gods, knowing good and evil (Genesis 3:4,5).*

While God's prohibitions were designed to protect and preserve them, the serpent planted seeds of doubt, distrust, fear, and unbelief in the woman. He also enticed her to obtain something apart from God by getting her to reason and appealing to her senses.

> *And when the woman saw that the tree was good for food, and that it was pleasant to the eyes, and a tree to be desired to make one wise, she took of the fruit thereof, and did eat, and gave also to her husband with her and he did eat (Genesis 3:6 emphasis added).*

And then something happened that changed the course of humanity.

> *And the eyes of them both were opened, and they knew they were naked: and they sewed fig leaves together, and made themselves aprons (Genesis 3:7 emphasis added).*

The woman disobeyed God by eating the fruit of the tree that God specifically told them not to eat. Despite God telling them the consequence, she ate the fruit, gave it to her husband, and he ate it. By doing so, they opened the door to fear and changed the course of humanity. In accepting the serpent's suggestion, the woman opened herself up to deception. When they ate, their eyes were opened, and they became aware of their nakedness and immediately sought to "cover" themselves up. Before they ate the fruit of the Tree of the Knowledge of Good and Evil, they were naked and unashamed. Once they ate the fruit, they became aware of their nakedness and were ashamed; they made fig leaves for aprons to cover up.

The opening of their eyes brought fear and shame. This first act of disobedience was the fruit of the tree of the knowledge of good and evil. When God called to Adam, He said, "Adam, where are you?"

Adam responded, "I heard Your Voice and was afraid because I was naked, so I hid myself."

God replied, "Who told you that you were naked?"

God did not call out to Adam because He couldn't locate him; He called out to Adam so that Adam could consider where he was. He had moved out of position, and God knew it. Their disobedience instantly brought an awareness of their defiance of God, and they hid out of fear. Instead of obeying out of reverential fear of God, they disobeyed and experienced the fear of God's punishment and wrath. This was never God's plan. While there are other consequences, fear has been one of the marks of man's fallen nature.

This still occurs today. Sin causes us to hide from the Presence of God and try to cover ourselves up. When we sin, there is deep within our knowledge that we have disobeyed God, and we experience feeling exposed, naked, and ashamed. We become afraid. We no longer reverence God; we just become afraid of His wrath and what He will do to us for having disobeyed. Disobedience and sin have fear and condemnation built in. If God is for you, who can be against you? But if God is against you, who can deliver you out of His hand? That is condemnation.

We don't want to face God, and out of pride, like Adam, we sew fig leaves together and try to cover up our sins. Instead, we should simply go to God, Who is the same yesterday, today, and forever, and seek forgiveness, fall on His mercy, and allow Him to restore us.

There was a season in my walk with the Lord when I fell into sin and paid a costly price. I was so afraid to face God that I shut my bible and walked away from God for over 10 years. See, I had gotten involved with a guy in college who I was with for over three years until I found out that he had been actively involved with another woman and was engaged to be married to her. To say I was devastated would be an understatement. To make things worse, he was a minister.

I believed that this was punishment for my sin and God's way of rejecting me, so I shut down and shut off my faith. It would take me over 10 years, trials, tests, multiple betrayals, public humiliation, and coming to the complete and total end of myself to reach back out to God and humble myself.

Matthew 21:44 says: "*And whosoever shall fall on this stone shall be broken: but on whomsoever it shall fall, it will grind him to powder.*" Let's just say that because of my pride, which turned to rebellion, the rock fell on me, and I was crushed—to powder. The Young's Literal Translations says: "… *it will crush him to pieces.*" We don't have to be crushed for God to show His mercy on us, but pride and hiding from God when in sin only deceives us into thinking God doesn't see our sin. We cannot hide from God. We also miss His grace and His mercy when we try to hide from Him.

In the previous chapter, we learned about some of God's attributes and His holy and righteous nature. To give context to the story of Adam and the fall of man, we understand that they fell, and humanity has suffered the consequence, but the truth is God is still good. He is just and merciful, has a plan of redemption for those who will enter into it, and this must be the foundation of all our understanding.

The serpent seduced the woman into disobedience and opened the door to fear. We no longer reverence God and obey Him out of faith and trust in who He is because we know His Nature, that He is good, and that He is for us.

Instead, after the fall, we became afraid for ourselves. We became self-focused, self-conscious, and prideful.

Our Adversary, the Devil, and Evil Spirits

The Bible makes it clear—we have an adversary. To understand and identify the adversary's role in fostering fear in our lives, we must properly understand who he is. In scripture, our adversary is described by several names—some proper, some improper.

- Lucifer, Satan, Devil, the Adversary
- Devil, demon
- Satan
- Serpent
- Dragon
- Enemy
- Accuser

The Hebrew word for serpent is *nachash*, meaning to hiss, whisper (a magic spell), to divine, enchanter, or enchantment. It can also mean to practice divination, observe omens, or to seek knowledge through divination. By now, you see where this revelation of the nature of the adversary is going. It is tied to the forbidden practice of the occult, which is obtaining supernatural knowledge through any means other than God. The fear of the Lord is the beginning of wisdom. God expressly forbade Israel from these satanic and demonic practices. Examples are:

- Leviticus 19:26
- Deuteronomy 18:10
- II Kings 17:17
- II Kings 21:6
- II Chronicles 33:6

In the Garden, Eve received "knowledge" from the serpent—divination. But God had forbidden the "knowledge" she received, which did not make her "wise" in the way she thought it would.

The devil is cunning and slick, and Scripture reveals

him as "more subtil" than all the other beasts of the field. The word subtil comes from the Hebrew word *aruwm*, meaning crafty or cunning in a negative sense, versus wise and prudent in a positive sense. It is the primitive root of the Hebrew word *aram,* meaning to be or to make bare, as in naked, to think, reveal or uncover. Sound familiar?

In his crafty nature, the serpent tricked the woman into thinking she would be wise and prudent by eating from the Tree of the Knowledge of Good and Evil. Instead, their eyes were only awakened to realize they were naked

The enemy uses this same trick of releasing deception by twisting knowledge and perverting it so that it is received in a way God never intended. This is why knowledge obtained apart from God is so dangerous.

When it comes from the occult, it is automatically tainted and brings bondage. God never intended them to know good and evil, but the enemy presented it as if there was some sinister motive on God's part to withhold from them.

Once Adam and Eve allowed the serpent to deceive them by attacking God's good nature, they became uncovered, were ashamed, and realized they were naked.

God had a plan for redemption, so we know how the story ends, but on the way, humanity has had to reckon with the consequences of the fall, and fear has become part and parcel of man's fallen state. It is not until Jesus Christ brought salvation that we could come to a reverential fear of the Lord and out of a perpetual fear of God's wrath.

Declaration:

Lord, I thank You that I can come before You naked and unashamed, and I don't have to hide from You because You cover my sin. I renounce the fear that entered through deception and disobedience—my own and those in my bloodline back to Adam, and I receive redemption through Christ to enter the fear of the Lord through the lens of Truth (Proverbs 14:26-27).

Chapter 5

The Judgment, Wrath, and Severity of God

Well; because of unbelief they were broken off,
and thou standest by faith. Be not highminded,
but fear: for if God spared not the natural
branches, take heed lest he also spare not thee.
Behold therefore the goodness and severity of
God: on them which fell, severity; but toward
thee, goodness, if thou continue in his good-
ness; otherwise thou also shalt be cut off.

Romans 11:20-22

The fear of the Lord is a righteous response to Who God Is—Holy. Reverential fear of God should lead us to desire to live righteous out of love and gratefulness towards Him. When we have a revelation of God's Nature and Character as holy, pure, just, and good, we can trust Him. When we forsake Him—His Word, His Will, and His Way—we risk His wrath. God's wrath is His Holy and righteous hatred and anger toward sin. Whereas our obedience demonstrates our reverential fear, our disobedience manifests fear of His wrath.

Reverential fear leads to loving devotion, honor, and respect because of Who God Is. Disobedience leads to consciousness of our failure and fear of what God will do because of it. It brings a realization that we have sinned, transgressed, and violated His Word. We become self-fo-cused, fearing punishment, being exposed, and feeling condemnation. This also leads to pride, which rejects and rebels against God, leading us further away from the Lord.

In the story I shared in the last chapter about God's dealing with me concerning the ungodly relationship that I was in, I experienced firsthand God's jealousy and wrath against the sin of idolatry. When we say that we receive God and His lordship, He takes us at our word because of His Holy Nature. I could not understand how I found myself in a situation where I thought I was the one and only in this person's life, only to find out I was "the side chick."

It was as if God pulled back the curtain on both our sin, and I was left naked and ashamed. It was God's judgment on the sin to allow me to be hurt and expose it. Because I didn't understand His Holy Nature, I just hid. And I had no fig leaf to cover me. My only choice was to fall on God's mercy. But because I did not know His mercy, I did not avail myself of it, and I went into darkness for many years, but I would come into the light of Christ much later.

When we don't properly understand the Holy Nature of God, we mistake His wrath and judgment of sin as hatred toward us. Only when we so identify with that which He hates do we experience His judgment as rejection and hatred of us. Because of God's Holy and righteous nature, He judges sin and does so out of love. We can't wrap our minds around a God who would respond in ways that seem severe because we don't know His nature.

He is not only sovereign but all-knowing, good, and just. We can best believe that if God causes or allows something to happen, He is just. If God judges, we can trust that it is justified. Period.

Let no man deceive you with vain words; for because of these things cometh the wrath of God upon the children of disobedience. "*Be not ye therefore partakers with them*" (Ephesians 5:6).

Christ came as the remedy for the wrath of God against sin and to redeem mankind from the eternal consequences of sin. He did not come to do away with the standards of holiness and righteousness that are integral to God's nature but to fulfill them.

For the Law was given by Moses, but grace and truth came by Jesus Christ (John 1:17).

Jesus is our example.

> *Think not that I am come to destroy the law, or the prophets; I am not come to destroy, but to fulfil (Matthew 5:17).*

The Law had to be fulfilled with truth. Jesus came so we would know the truth and have the grace to walk in it. In this revelation, we can know God, Who He Is, have a proper perspective of Him based on truth, and have the divine power of Holy Spirit working in us to fulfill the Word. We fulfill the Word just as Christ fulfilled the law.

This is why Christ died for us, so we may appropriate the sacrifice He made to get us back into right standing with God, position us as sons, and reconcile us to the Father. Jesus didn't just die to get us out of trouble with God. He died to give us a new nature and new life whereby we no longer have a sin nature.

Holy Spirit can bring us back into alignment when we sin and give us the power to resist sin and live holy. Holy Spirit gives us new desires so that we no longer desire to sin but have a thirst and hunger for righteousness. This allows us to leave behind the old nature that follows the course of the god of this age, the devil, and his nature.

> *He that committeth sin is of the devil; for the devil sinneth from the beginning. For this purpose, the Son of God is manifested, that he might destroy the works of the devil (1 John 3:8).*

Before we received Christ, we were in darkness, and our nature was to sin.

And you hath he quickened, who were dead in trespasses and sins; wherein in time past ye walked according to the course of this world, according to the prince of the power of the air, the spirit that now worketh in the children of disobedience: among whom also we all had our conversation in times past in the lusts of our flesh, fulfilling the desires of the flesh and of the mind; and were by nature the children of wrath, even as others. But God who is rich in mercy, for his great love wherewith he loved us, even when we were dead in sins, hath quickened us together with Christ, (by grace ye are saved;) and hath raised us up together and made us sit together in heavenly places in Christ Jesus; that in the ages to come he might shew the exceeding riches of his grace in his kindness toward us through Christ Jesus (Ephesians 2:1-7).

We lived our lives according to the desires of our flesh and the sinful lusts of our carnal nature until Christ came, and we received him. Before then, we were slaves to sin, and we were under God's wrath.

For the wrath of God is revealed from Heaven against all ungodliness and unrighteousness of men who hold the truth in unrighteousness, because that which may be known of God is manifest in them; for God hath shewed it unto them. For the invisible things of him from the creation of the world are clearly seen, being understood by the things that are made, even his eternal power and Godhead; so that they are without excuse; because that, when they knew God, they glorified him not as God, neither were thankful; but became vain in their imaginations, and their foolish heart was darkened (Romans 1:18-21).

> *...who knowing the judgment of God, that they which commit such things are worthy of death, not only do the same but have pleasure in them that do them (Romans 1:32).*

These scriptures show that God revealed Himself to man. Because they were not thankful but began to follow after their darkened hearts and became foolish, He gave them over to their lusts to receive the payment for their waywardness—perversion, corruption, and condemnation.
There are consequences built into sin. They would receive what was coming to them, the fruit of their sin, the wrath of God, and ultimately separation from God and death.

> *Be not deceived; God is not mocked; for whatsoever a man soweth, that shall he also reap. For he that soweth to his flesh shall of the flesh reap corruption; but he that soweth to the Spirit shall of the Spirit reap life everlasting (Galatians 6:7-9).*

The Word is clear. God has made Himself known to man, and we have within us the knowledge of Him, His Holiness, and His wrath against sin. When we forsake the fear of the Lord and enter into pride, carnality, and rebellion, it leads to sin. We then open the door to perversion and provoke God to judgment. If we sow to our flesh, we are sowing into death. When we sin, we know that we are wrong. But when we live a life of sin, our conscience gets seared, so we are no longer convicted of sin. It becomes a downward spiral where deception sets in, delusion follows, and we can become dead in sins.

Disobeying God and practicing sin distorts our view. Before Adam and Eve fell, they were naked and unashamed before God. Once they disobeyed and their "eyes" were opened, they hid themselves because their nakedness now caused them to feel exposed. They felt shame and the need to cover themselves up. The aprons they made to cover their nakedness were made of fig leaves. They now had a perverted view of their nakedness based on having sinned.

God asked them, "Who told you that you were naked?" Their view of God had now been distorted because of their distorted view of their nakedness. The serpent took advantage of their innocence by planting seeds that twisted God's intentions and accused His character.

Prayer:

Lord, thank You for giving me a proper perspective of Your judgment and wrath and the severity that comes from Your Holy and righteous Nature. Help me to reverence and honor You in Your judgment of sin. I declare that sin will have no dominion over me and that I recognize Your hate for sin and know that it is because of Your love toward me. (Romans 11:22)

Chapter 6

Reconciling the Goodness and the Severity of God

The Lord is not slack concerning his promise, as some men count slackness; but is longsuffering to us-ward, not willing that any should perish, but that all should come to repentance.

2 Peter 3:9

The goodness and mercy of God are not contradicted by His severity. The Topical Bible describes severity as: "(n) gravity or austerity; extreme strictness; rigor, harshness; as, the severity of a reprimand or a reproof; severity of discipline or government; exactness. The word severity comes from the Greek word *apotomia,* meaning sharpness, and *apotomos*, meaning abruptly, curtly" (p. 2076).

It may be difficult to reconcile how God could be said to be good yet respond in sharp, cutting, harsh, or abrupt ways. His Holy nature demands a righteous response to sin. Because He is love, He is provoked to anger by sin and unrighteousness. His severity is His expression of His righteous indignation, and it is good. There is no justice without judgment. God sets things right when they are out of order, and it is good for Him to respond accordingly. Realizing that His severity is entirely consistent with His Holy nature will help us not to be discouraged when He corrects us in ways that seem hard or harsh. God cares about our feelings but will not spare them if we violate His Holy nature.

Ye have not yet resisted unto blood, striving against sin. And ye have forgotten the exhortation which speaketh unto you as unto children,

My son, despise not thou the chastening of the Lord, Nor faint when thou art rebuked of him: for whom the Lord loveth he chasteneth, And scourgeth every son whom he receiveth (Hebrews 12:4-6).

While God is good and kind, He must bring things back into His divine order. That's why He sent Jesus to restore and reconcile us back to Him and not only people, the human race and mankind but all of creation.

And having made peace through the blood of his cross, <u>by him to reconcile all things unto himself;</u> by him, I say whether they be things in earth, or things in heaven (Colossians 1:20 emphasis added).

God's ultimate plan is to restore all things to His original intent. Because of the fall of mankind, His heavy hand is sometimes necessary to deal with man's stubborn heart. If we are indeed His children and have the reverential fear of the Lord, then we receive His rebuke as love, not rejection. Part of the distortion resulting from disobedience and sin is misunderstanding God's intentions and motives in His wrath, severity, and judgment.

These three attributes of His Holy nature are necessary to see justice, righteousness, and truth in the earth. If we have a proper perspective of God's Nature as a good God, we do not faint or lose heart when He corrects us or deals with us in our disobedience. When we experience that side of Him, it will bring conviction and correction, not condemnation. As sons of God, we have redemption through Christ, so His judgment is never condemning; it is redemptive. It brings us back into divine alignment with His will and purpose.

For this reason, we reverence God and don't have to fear His wrath when He responds in righteousness to sin. We are redeemed, and so we experience His mercy. We obey out of love for Him and not because we are afraid of His wrath.

Honor and respect for God's wrath are always in order. We do not want to mock God or provoke Him.

To mock Him is to test His patience or to act irreverently toward His holiness. This is foolish. His kindness and love should never cause us to think we can practice sin and habitually disobey or defy Him without consequences. God's delayed response is His mercy, not His passive acceptance of sin.

Prayer:

Lord, I will not despise Your chastening nor faint when You correct me. Because I fear and reverence You, I receive Your rebukes in love and know that they are for my good that I would have a pure and righteous nature. (Hebrews 12:5; Proverbs 3:11)

Chapter 7

Spirit of Fear, Fear of Man, and Fear of Evil

For God hath not given us a spirit of fear, but of power and of love and of a sound mind.

2 Timothy 1:7

We often quote this scripture as a reminder not to be fearful. However, verse 6 gives us a context for Paul's exhortation to his spiritual son Timothy.

> *Wherefore I put thee in remembrance that thou stir up the gift of God, which is in thee by the putting on of my hands. For God hath not given us the spirit of fear; but of power, and of love, and of a sound mind (2 Timothy 1:6-7).*

The exhortation contained in this verse was about not being timid about operating in the gifts God has given us. We don't have faint hearts because Christ is in us and has given us Holy Spirit, Who empowers and emboldens us to walk out our call. A spirit of fear is a disposition that is fearful, timid, and insecure. This is not the spirit God has given us, but it is power through Holy Spirit, the Love of God, and a mind that is sharp, focused, and able to correctly filter our thoughts and discern experiences so that we see and interpret things accurately. We are powerful, and love gives us confidence and security to go forth.

There is also a battle for our minds because this is where the war is waged to get us to go one way or another, specifically, away from the things of God.

The weapons of our warfare are not carnal but mighty through God to the pulling down of strong-holds, casting down imaginations and every high thing that exalts itself against the knowledge of God and bringing into captivity every thought to the obedience of Christ. And having a readiness to revenge all disobedience when our obedience is fulfilled (2 Corinthians 10:4-6).

A negative stronghold is a fortified place in our minds that guards it from truth. It affects our ability to see things correctly and have the proper perspective of God and who we are in Him. We can also fortify our minds with strongholds of truth that guard against deception.

And be not conformed to this world: but be ye transformed by the renewing of your mind, that ye may prove what is that good, and acceptable, and perfect, will of God (Romans 12:2).

For we wrestle not against flesh and blood, but against principalities, against powers, against the rulers of darkness of this world, against spiritual wickedness in high places (Ephesians 6:12).

This points to two essential truths:
- **Our battle is spiritual, and our weapons are spiritual.**
- **The battle is in our minds.**

When we are obedient to God and set our hearts in devotion to Him, He works in us to will and to do His good pleasure (Philippians 2:13). When we disobey, the enemy of our souls uses our rebellion to gain access to our minds to draw us deeper into darkness. The Bible reminds us that we all have had our turn walking in this disobedience.

"And you hath he quickened, who were dead in

trespasses and sins; wherein in time past ye walked according to the course of this world, according to the prince of the power of the air, the spirit that now worketh in the children of disobedience; among whom also we all had our conversation in times past in the lusts of our flesh, fulfilling the desires of the flesh and the mind; and were by nature the children of wrath, even as others (Ephesians 2:1-3).

Conversation is not just dialogue. The word used by apostle Paul refers to our walk, how we conduct ourselves, our lifestyle. Before we came to Christ, we all lived a lifestyle of disobedience. Therefore, we were children of wrath—we were under God's judgment and condemnation, deserving of eternal damnation. Once we came to Christ and our calling and election were made sure, and we came to learn our gifts, mantles, and assignments; we were confirmed, given a stamp of approval, and then pronounced and commissioned to go forth in the work God has given us.

We can walk confidently in our gifts to fulfill our assignment. We no longer feel timid or insecure because we have Heaven's confirmation and backing. We have the power to carry out our assignment, love (the gifts operate by love) and the sober mind that gives us stability to walk in our call.

Fear of Man

The fear of man bringeth a snare, But he whoso putteth his trust in the Lord shall be safe (Proverbs 29:25).

There is a fear of man that masquerades as honor, but it is a false honor. Similarly, there is a "wisdom" that is actually fear masquerading as prudence and good judgment. These are both ways that fear can trick us into thinking that we are doing something noble by respecting man when we are really operating in idolatry or that we are "protecting" ourselves when we are really allowing fear to rule. We must discern this, hold our hearts up to the Word of God, and allow Holy Spirit to expose this deception when it is in operation.

> *The Lord is on my side; I will not fear: what can man do to me? (Psalm 118:6).*

The fear of man is often manifested in a false sense of honor, fear of what man can do, be it real or imagined. We fear man when we will not tell man the truth, obey man rather than God, and choose our way over God's way. This is fear and idolatry. There have been times in my walk with God when the fear of man was so strong in my life. I would tremble to do the will of God, speak a Word from the Lord, or become so fearful of man that I would disobey God to avoid consequences from man. This torment would follow me for many seasons until I would simply purpose in my heart to obey God regardless of the consequences of man. The idolatry of man was hard to break, but the Lord brought me through and out by prayer, fasting, and consecration. I was more concerned with what man would do than God. Praise the Lord for deliverance!

It is not unusual to obey man rather than God, but... *"We ought to obey God rather than men"* (Acts 5:29). Peter and the disciples made up their minds that, because they feared the Lord, they would obey God rather than obey man. And they paid for it. This is a harsh reality of fearing the Lord and living for Him. You cannot fear man. You may find yourself having to take a stand for the things of God, and it may cost you. Persecution comes to those who choose Christ, but God is with us.

> *I, even I, am He who comforts you. Who are you that thou should be afraid of a man who will die, and of the son of a man who will be made like grass (Isaiah 51:12 NKJV).*

Scripture is clear: we are not to fear man. Our reverential

fear is exclusively for God. If we fear, reverence, or look to appease man, we have made man an idol. There is an appropriate honor and respect that we give to man, but if we find ourselves disobeying God or sinning to appease others, we will surely arouse God's anger. God is a jealous God. His jealousy is not like man's. He has a rightful expectation of fidelity and faithfulness to Him as our Creator and the only true living God. Fear of rejection or harm by men should never lead us to sin or disobey God.

Sadly, many of us who claim to belong to Christ have found ourselves at one time or another in the snare of the fear of man. A snare is a type of trap set to cause one's foot to get caught and prevent them from moving. We cannot move forward in the things of God if we are trapped and ensnared in men-pleasing. Seeking man's approval, trying to gain man's favor, or avoiding rejection or disapproval is idolatry.

God has declared, *"Ye shall have no other gods before Me"* (Exodus 20:3). This means no other being is to have the worship that only belongs to God. We owe our reverential fear and awe to God, not some idol. He is our Source of divine provision and protection; when we trust Him, we are safe. We cannot say we trust in God but are afraid of man.

The Jews of Jesus' day, although they believed in His teachings, would not speak openly about Him because they feared the religious leaders kicking them out of the synagogue.

> *Howbeit, no man spake openly of him for fear of the Jews (John 7:13).*

> *And fear not them which kill the body, but are not able to kill the soul: but rather fear him which is able to destroy both soul and body in hell (Matthew 10:28).*

> *Whosoever, therefore, shall confess me before men, him will I confess also before my Father which is*

in heaven. But whosoever shall deny me before men, him will I also deny before my Father which is in heaven (Matthew 10: 32 -33).

Fear of man can often look like:
- Avoidance
- Dishonesty or withholding truth to appease man
- Flattery
- Man-pleasing
- Disobeying God to avoid consequences from man
- Compromise

It is not uncommon to find oneself men-pleasing. We have all been guilty before and even in our walk with the Lord of allowing men to lead us away from the things of God into sin. This happens when we lack the fear of the Lord. We can also use others to get what we want, becoming men-pleasers, desiring selfish gain, or for self-preservation. God never created us to fear another person. When we set our gaze and affection upon the Lord, our perspective of people and our view of God changes.

Recognizing God is all-powerful, good, and loves us gives us the proper view of God. Have you ever been afraid to tell someone that "God told me to do it"? I have, and God exposed this as idolatry, and I had to go into deeper levels of surrender to walk in the fear of the Lord so that I could boldly declare my obedience to God even in the face of losing favor with man.

God is a Jealous God!

But ye shall destroy their altars, break their images, and cut down their groves: for thou shalt worship no other god: for the Lord whose name is Jealous is a jealous God (Exodus 34:13-14).

The Hebrew word for jealous is *qanna*. It means to express strong emotion in which the object is desirous of some aspect of possession of the object. This describes God's posture toward us but is also characteristic of His zeal. It is His intolerance of unfaithfulness and hostility toward any rival of our affection and devotion that is due rightly to Him alone. In His zealousness and jealousy for His people, He protects them from their enemies and avenges them.

His jealousy is not like man's. We have no claim to another person except in a covenant marriage, whereby we expect faithfulness and fidelity. But God's jealousy is righteous and pure, not merely self-serving. It is out of His love for His creation. Man's jealousy manifests as anger and is characteristic of the carnal nature of man that often leads to wickedness and can become demonic (James 3:14–16).

God's zeal for us is holy, righteous, and born out of His pure nature and desire for His people. Because He is jealous for us, He rightfully expects our devotion. Like a husband to a wife, the covenant of marriage comes with the expectation that one's full and complete devotion be to the other. When it is not, it arouses a zeal and jealousy to protect their right of possession of the other, not as property but as the one to whom is owed the fulfillment of the covenant vow to be faithful and devoted exclusively.

We owe our absolute devotion exclusively to God. Our worship, our obedience, and our love are all owed to Him. When we begin to give anyone or anything else that which is due only to God, we have become idolaters, and God will not tolerate idolatry.

> *I am the Lord thy God, which brought thee out of the land of Egypt, out of the house of bondage. Thou shalt have no other gods before me (Exodus 20:2-3).*

Fear of Evil

Psalm 23 describes the faithfulness of God as a Shepherd and Keeper of His sheep. The picture is one of sheep being led to lie down in a green pasture, to rest beside still waters, walking with the Shepherd, guiding them, and keeping them safe from the hazards of the journey of life. He describes a leader, comforter, keeper, and protector. Though he walks through places where death casts a shadow, he will not fear because the Shepherd is with him, and he is comforted by the Shepherd's ability to keep and protect him from evil.

> *Yea, though I walk through the valley of the shadow of death, I will fear no evil for thou art with me; Thy rod and thy staff they comfort me (Psalm 23:4).*

When we fear evil, we do not trust God. We must, therefore, renew our minds with the Word so that it becomes that fortified place where the truth keeps us from the fear of evil.

When we wholeheartedly trust in the Lord, we have confidence that He will protect us. When left to our own devices, fear can set in and cause us to attempt to preserve ourselves. We are no match for the devil without Jesus Christ, our Shepherd.

We are encouraged to renew our minds so that we are transformed into the image of Christ and prove and demonstrate Him on earth. We surrender our carnal lives to Him so that Christ can manifest through Holy Spirit in our lives. This happens by replacing wrong thinking patterns with the Word of God.

> *Be not conformed to this world but be transformed by the renewing of the mind (Romans 12:2).*

We then have the mind of Christ, where our thoughts are of things that are:

> *Finally, brethren, whatsoever things are true, whatsoever things are honest, whatsoever things are just, whatsoever things are pure, whatsoever things are lovely, whatsoever things are of good*

report; if there be any virtue, and if there be any praise, think on these things (Philippians 4:8).

This is our guidance on what to keep our minds on. But when we are not vigilant or maintain a posture of obedience to the Lord, we leave the door of our hearts open to the enemy. He uses fear to keep us in bondage to darkness, bringing all manner of fear and evil foreboding. He brings thoughts and imaginations to our minds to keep us in constant fear. But this is what the Bible says about Satan.

I beheld Satan as lightning fall from heaven (Luke 10:18).

The once-anointed cherub Lucifer, who rose up in pride and was cast out of heaven, who took one-third of the angels with him, exists in the second heaven as the god of this age, the cosmos, the world system. Satan is referred to as:
- **The prince of the power of the air**
- **The god of this world**
- **The accuser**

Satan and his horde of fallen angels, demons, and imps hate humanity. Because we are made in the image of God, he hates us. Because he gained control of the earth/world through Adam's sin, he fashioned the world and its systems to be anti-Christ. He wanted to remove any trace of God, our Creator, and remove Him from our hearts and minds. Satan's primary weapon is deception, and fear is his ammunition.

He does not do his work alone but uses a demonic and diabolical army he has at his disposal. Evil spirits gain access to the hearts and minds of people, bringing them into captivity to do their will. They have been relegated to darkness; they operate in darkness. Therefore, when we are in darkness, that is—
- **Deception**
- **Disobedience**
- **Rebellion**

- Wickedness
- Perverseness
- Confusion
- Willful ignorance

We come under the authority of the powers of darkness. They have full access to oppress, suppress, bind, occupy, and possess our souls and work all manner of evil in the earth, causing those who don't know God to be constantly afraid.

If we belong to Jesus, evil spirits can't possess us, but they can oppress and operate through us if we are not vigilant about staying close to the Lord. They can use these places of darkness as a means of agreement to get us out of the will of God and do their bidding.

Prayer:
Lord, forgive me for allowing timidity to keep me from embracing and operating in the gifts and the call on my life. Lord, I choose to walk in the fear of the Lord; the fear of man and what he can do to me have no place in me. I declare that You have given me the spirit of power, love, and a sound mind. I will not fear evil because I know You are with me and for me. (1 Timothy 1:7; Psalm 27:1; Psalm 23:4)

Chapter 8

Cowardice, Courage, Boldness, and Confidence

The wicked flee when no man pursueth: But the righteous are bold as a lion.

Proverbs 28:1

Throughout Scripture, The Lord encourages us not to be afraid. In encounters with His people, whether directly or through an angel, He told them to "*fear not*" or "*do not be afraid*." This exhortation is given 365 times in the Bible. That tells us that God is aware of our propensity to become afraid, and He dealt directly with their fear, telling them not to be afraid.

God does not want a relationship with His people in which we are afraid *of* Him. But until our knowledge and revelation of the love of God mature, our first reaction to the Presence of God may be to be afraid. If God has not given us the spirit of fear, where does it come from? This is the fear that is not reverential of God but manifests as:

- **Fright**
- **Terror**
- Panic
- **Anxiety**
- **Paranoia**
- Avoidance
- **Apprehension**
- Silence
- **Timidity**
- **Insecurity**

Common fears include fear of:
- Dying
- Failure
- Speaking
- Evil
- Failure
- Success
- Confrontation
- Rejection
- Lack
- Man
- The unknown

> *The Lord is my light and my salvation, whom shall I fear? The Lord is the strength of my life; of whom shall I be afraid? (Psalm 27:1)*

When we have a reverential fear of the Lord and have a revelation of His Holiness and omnipotence, we don't fear anything else because we know that the One who is all-powerful is on our side.

> *What shall we then say to these things? If God be for us, who can be against us? (Romans 8:31)*

> *There shall no man be able to stand before you: for the Lord your God shall lay the fear of you and the dread of you upon all the land that ye shall tread upon, as he hath said unto you (Deuteronomy 11:25).*

God is on our side, so we need not fear a man—for any reason.

> *Who shall lay anything to the charge of God's elect? It is God that justifieth (Romans 8:33).*

No weapon that is formed against thee shall pros-
per; and every tongue that shall rise against thee
in judgment thou shall condemn. This is the her-
itage of the servants of the Lord, and their righ-
teousness is of me, saith the Lord (Isaiah 54:17).

What a powerful declaration of truth! These verses should cause us to shout for joy as they prove that we have the backing of the Lord of Heaven and earth when faced with accusations and attacks against our character and who we are in God. Judgments come from people, Satan, the accuser, and even from ourselves. These are the tongues that rise against us. They can release evil decrees, curses, evil tidings, and judgments meant to label us and attack our character and identity in Christ. Accusations are railed against us to bring condemnation, to discourage and defeat us. These weapons are formed constantly, but the Word says, "… thou shall condemn." This means that they won't be able to prosper because of who we are because our righteousness is of God. If we stand on God's righteousness and not our own, judgments levied against us have no power; they fail and are indeed condemned.

If you need more proof, see 2 Corinthians 5:21:

For he hath made him to be sin for us, who knew no sin; that we might be made the righteousness of God in him.

Yea, though I walk through the valley of the
shadow of death, I will fear no evil, for thou art
with me, Thy rod and thy staff they comfort me
(Psalm 23:4).

There are times when death may cast a shadow over our lives, and the threat may be very real. However, Psalm 23 reminds us that God is our protector, so we don't have to fear evil. There is much fear in the world today. Evil tidings are repeated daily as news reports constantly remind us of all the death and destruction at work in the earth. It is no wonder many are afraid. Afraid to go out, afraid to live life, afraid to speak the truth—just fearful of life itself. But the Lord tells us He has overcome the world, so we don't need to fear evil. He never promises us that our lives will be free of trouble. He tells us that we will have tribulation in this world but that He has overcome the world (John 16:33).

Cowardice

> *But the fearful, and unbelieving, and the abominable, and murderers, whoremongers, and sorcerers, idolaters, and all liars, shall have their part in the lake which burneth with fire and brimstone, which is the second death (Revelation 21:8).*

Why does the Lord include the cowardly and the fearful alongside murderers and sexually immoral as having their part in the lake of fire? Because cowardice, like other sins, is an affront to His nature. In shrinking back in fear, the cowardly find themselves entangled in sin. Cowards protect themselves, frequently at the expense or to the detriment of others. A person who doesn't speak up or act when it requires them to put their self-interest on the line is a coward. Cowards don't speak up when they witness violence, injustice, or when another person's name is maligned because they don't want the backlash or persecution.

Cowards can often contribute to another person's violation by refusing to act courageously. There are laws that criminalize bystander behavior, as well as professional standards of conduct that include the duty to warn or inform. Moral, ethical, legal, and professional duty exist even in the natural. Being afraid is not an excuse.

Cowardice is acting out of fear to protect oneself from real or perceived danger or harm. This is why God took issue with cowards because their fear would cause them to act in their own interest to the detriment of others. My personal struggle with cowardice was borne out of sin and iniquity in my bloodline as well as the perpetuation of sin and transgressions in my life. I was afraid to act in obedience to God out of fear for my own personal welfare. It is absolutely miserable to be fearful, so much so that you won't speak up or act to preserve someone else for fear for your own life. Fear is an absolute prison, one that only a revelation of the love of God and reverential fear of the Lord can free you. This is part of my testimony and what led me to release this book.

In Judges 7, the first soldiers God had Gideon send home from the battlefield were the fearful; 22,000 of the 32,000 left because they feared, leaving 10,000 men in Gideon's army. Shakespeare's Julius Caesar speaks these often-quoted words: *"A coward dies a thousand deaths, the valiant taste of death but once."* For the fearful, every situation presents a threat and fear of death.

Those who act cowardly do not fear the Lord. If they feared the Lord, they would be more afraid to dishonor or disobey Him than they would be of their circumstances. Cowards will:

- **Lie**
- **Deny**
- **Betray**
- **Be silent**
- **Be two-faced**
- **Be men-pleasers**
- **Shrink back**
- **Run**
- **Back down**
- **Shift responsibility**
- **Blame**
- **Be selfish**
- **Support in secret**

Cowards are not only fearful, but they are also prideful and selfish. They are likely betrayers of God, others, and even themselves. They are deceived into trusting their fears to close ranks around them and keep them safe. Cowardice breeds compromise, hypocrisy, and men-pleasing. Cowardice and fear are forms of pride because they are self-focused.

There are many examples of men in the Bible—including men who did great exploits in God's Name—who exhibited fear and cowardice:

- **Peter was found to be a coward and a man-pleaser by not wanting to be seen with the disciples.**
- **Peter denied Jesus three times.**
- **Abraham and Isaac were fearful and lied about their wives being their sisters and allowing them to be taken.**
- **Some of the religious leaders of Israel believed in Jesus but would not openly confess it because they feared being put out of the synagogue by the Pharisees.**

Contrast these with Paul, Silvanus, and Timothy, who were applauded for their steadfastness and faith even while enduring all their afflictions and persecutions. (2 Thessalonians 1: 1-12).

The fear of the Lord, following Christ, and standing for the Kingdom of God necessitates courage, confidence, and boldness. We hold the truth in Christ Jesus, so we must take a stand in the face of lies, injustice, wickedness, and opposition. Persecutions and afflictions will come to the true believer and the truly converted. Those who claim Christ will be tested. The cowardly will not be able to stand in the evil day when this test comes.

> *Whosoever shall seek to save his life shall lose it; and whosoever shall lose his life shall preserve it (Luke 17:33).*

The Bible clearly states that if we want to preserve our lives, we must be willing to lose it. This means we must be prepared to lose all so that we may gain the life that Christ died for us to have in this life and the one to come. Losing our lives looks like not being afraid of what people will say or think about us for speaking and living the truth, not being concerned about our reputations, and putting our life's plans and agendas aside to live for Christ.

But how often have we cowered in silence rather than stand up or speak up because we feared a negative consequence? Many feared what the "Pharisees," the religious or political leaders, would say.

We fear losing favor or privilege with people, systems, and institutions. We fear losing power, position, and money. We fear losing our reputations and sometimes our lives—which can all be real threats. But sonship demands not just allegiance but faithful devotion and honor to God. We must stand on the side of the Lord. There is no gray area, no fence to straddle, or thin line to walk on. This is a hard reality but one we must reckon with. Jesus was obedient unto death. Here is what the Lord commands:

- **Be strong and courageous (Joshua 1:9)**
- **Strive for the truth unto death (Ecclesiastes 4:28)**
- **Choose this day whom ye will serve (Joshua 24:15)**
- **Don't be afraid of their faces, or I will confound you before them (Jeremiah 1:8-9)**

Courage, Boldness, and Confidence

The Lord is my light and my salvation; whom shall I fear? The Lord is the strength of my life; of whom shall I be afraid? (Psalm 27:1)

God created us, Jesus saved us, and Holy Spirit keeps us day by day. So we can trust that God will be faithful to us.

Casting all your care upon Him; for He careth for you (1 Peter 5:7).

The Lord will perfect that which concerneth me: Thy mercy, O Lord, endureth forever: Forsake not the works of thine own hands (Psalm 138:8).

But seek ye first the kingdom of God, and His

righteousness; and all these things shall be added unto you (Matthew 6:33).

So, all that we try to protect and preserve ourselves from, God has already made provision. When man fell into sin, God made provision for our salvation. When we come into the knowledge of our sonship, we can rest in His completed work. He told us that in His Word.

These things I have spoken unto you, that in me ye might have peace. In the world ye shall have tribulation: but be of good cheer; I have overcome the world (John 16:3).

Be strong and of a good courage, fear not, nor be afraid of them: for the Lord thy God, he it is that doth go with thee; he will not fail thee, nor forsake thee (Deuteronomy 31:6).

Be careful for nothing; but in every thing by prayer and supplication with thanksgiving let your request be made known unto God. And the peace of God which passeth all understanding shall keep your hearts and minds through Christ Jesus (Philippians 4:6-7).

Have not I commanded thee? Be strong and of a good courage; be not afraid, neither be thou dismayed; for the Lord thy God is with thee whithersoever thou goest (Joshua 1:9).

Fear is a byproduct of unbelief. When we reject the truth of the Gospel, we enter darkness where fear can reign. Unbelief can also lead to complacency—a smug sense of self-satisfaction or safety while unaware of present danger. The fact is without Jesus, there is much to fear. Jesus is the Word Made Flesh (John 1:14) and the expressed image of God (Colossians 1:15). To believe in Him and receive the sacrifice Jesus made on the cross for our sin with His life is to enter the promises and provision of God—the Truth.

The more you embrace truth, the more you get to know God, the more your confidence grows. As your confidence grows, your courage to face adversity, persecution, and attacks from the enemy increases. Not only that, but you can also speak boldly and declare your faith. This is why seeking God, studying the Bible, and practicing spiritual disciplines like meditating on scripture, praying, fasting, and applying the Word to your life are essential.

> *Let us therefore come boldly unto the throne of grace, that we may obtain mercy, and find grace to help in time of need (Hebrews 4:16).*

In confidence and boldness, we approach God. We don't come to God prideful and brazen, but in humility and reverential fear, and entreat Him as our Heavenly Father. We know He will hear and answer us because of Who He Is, His goodness, holiness, and His Love for us. Our confidence in God also emboldens us to declare that He is God, Jesus is Lord, and openly confess Him and proclaim the Gospel. The more we draw close to God, seek His Presence, and His Word, the more our confidence grows, and this confidence in the Lord produces courage.

> *The wicked flee when no man pursueth, But the righteous are bold as a lion (Proverbs 28:1).*

Righteousness breeds boldness. Wicked people have to look over their shoulders and are constantly on guard for their lives – even when no one is after them.

The word courage comes from the Hebrew word *keras,*"meaning 'horn.' The horn in Hebrew culture is a symbol of strength. The Greek word is *hupostasis*, which means steadfastness of mind, firmness, and resolution. Courage has to do with the heart. It is not always the absence of fear, but courage acts in the face of fear. Throughout the Bible, the Lord often exhorts His people to "be courageous."

Conversely, the Greek word for discourage is *sunthrupto*, meaning to break in pieces, to crush; to deprive of strength, to dispirit. It also means to incapacitate, to be fainthearted, and to be weary. This is what fear does and often how the enemy of our souls comes to break us down through attacks against our faith and to discourage us from entering the things of God.

> *And from the days of John the Baptist until now, the kingdom of heaven suffereth violence, and the violent take it by force (Matthew 11:12).*

The fear of the Lord brings about knowledge and understanding. When we know Him as Father, as sons, we have confidence and, therefore, boldness when it comes to the things of God. We don't come from a place of entitlement, but we have confidence as sons that we have an inheritance. We know our place as sons and daughters so we can approach God and lay claim on His promises. Or we can stand boldly and confidently to defend the Kingdom because we have assurance of His promises. We have standing and authority to demand the enemy to loose, cease, and desist and see him retreat.

> *Submit yourselves, therefore, to God. Resist the devil, and he will flee from you (James 4:7).*

Holy Spirit's role in instilling courage in us is that of Comforter. To be comforted is to be reassured or to have confidence restored in the face of discouragement. Circumstances come to bring discouragement and break our confidence in God. Holy Spirit, the Spirit of Truth, leads us into all truth. Discouragement often comes in the form of distortions, deception, and lies from external forces or even internal mindsets. Scripture reminds us:

- Holy Spirit leads us into all truth (John 16:13)

- Satan is the father of lies (John 8:44)
- We must renew our minds so that we may be transformed (Romans 12:2)
- We must pull down strongholds in our minds and bring our thoughts captive to the obedience of Christ (2 Corinthians 10:4-6)
- There is a spirit of error (1 John 4:6)

All this means there is a danger of falling into deception and error. We must war against the thoughts and belief systems that have become strongholds in our minds that keep us from walking in truth. We go to war with them by renewing our minds and allowing Holy Spirit—the Spirit of Truth—to bring us out of error into truth. In addition, we need Holy Spirit because He empowers us to resist sin and alerts us when we are entering into deception. Holy Spirit works with our conscience to trigger an internal alarm when something is "off" or "isn't right." We learn to heed the promptings of the Holy Spirit by embarking upon our walk with God and learning His Voice.

We don't want to dismiss the nudges of Holy Spirit because this is where we receive warnings that protect us from unseen dangers. He is also called the Spirit of Grace and the Spirit of Wisdom, so He is aware at all times of all factors at work everywhere. He is right 1000% of the time, and we can trust His wisdom, but we must learn to hear His Voice and follow His guidance.

Howbeit when he, the Spirit of Truth, is come, he will guide you into all truth (John 16:13).

When we truly grasp this truth and hide it in our hearts, we will have the confidence we need to live a bold and uncompromising life in the Lord. When we hold the truth of Who God IS and put our faith and trust in Him alone, we have the confidence to face life with courage and boldness. When all else is shaken, we remain steadfast, unmovable, and unshaken.

Declaration:

I am not a coward, but I am bold, and my confidence is in my God. I am bold as a lion because I am the righteousness of God in Christ Jesus. (Proverbs 28:1; 2 Corinthians 5:21)

Chapter 9

Pride, Idolatry, Sin, and Its Consequences

The fear of the Lord is to hate evil: Pride, and arrogancy, and the evil way, and the froward mouth, do I hate.

Proverbs 8:13

Pride is man without God.

When man attempts to rely on his own devices, it is pride, and it is deception. Pride says, "I can do everything without God, and therefore I don't need God."

This deception causes us to reject the very One Who Is all-sufficient. While we attempt to live without God, deep in us is the knowledge of our Creator's existence, and the disconnect creates apprehension, fear, and foreboding. Man has gotten so deep in pride, deception, and darkness he is deceived that he will never have anything to do with God. Thus, he has no fear of the Lord. However, the life he lives is not free of fear.

Pride is self-exaltation. Pride relies on self. Pride removes God from the equation. God is all-powerful, all-knowing, and ever-present. He is also Creator. "*The earth is the Lord's and the fullness thereof and they that dwell within*" (Psalm 24:1). He is sovereign and holds the sole authority and right to establish creation as He pleases. It is a direct affront to God to enter pride. Pride says, "Man is God."

Pride arouses God's anger and jealousy. God resists the proud and gives grace to the humble. Pride is a form of idolatry as it exalts man above God—when we sin, we allow our carnal nature to be exalted above God, Who Is

Holy. God will not share His glory with another, and His commandments are clear:

> *Thou shalt have no other gods before Me (Exodus 20:3).*

> *And thou shalt love the Lord thy God with all thine heart, with all thy soul, and with all thy might (Deuteronomy 6:5).*

When I was in my teens, I remember the first time, in my rebellion, staying out all night with my teenage boyfriend. There weren't cell phones back then, so checking in and tracking your child down was arduous. You would have to know where they were and have the number.

As the hours passed, I was afraid to call my mother and tell her I was alright. She would never have consented to my staying out all night, much less with my boyfriend. Yet I did it anyway out of disobedience to what I knew was right. My boyfriend and I wanted to indulge in sin, so we decided to sneak and spend the night together at his house. I didn't consider how worried my mother would be about me and the fear she might have wondered if something bad had happened to me. Of course, I couldn't even enjoy my little "sneak time" as I spent the entire night fearing the trouble I would be in when I got home.

I knew I would have to face the consequences. I felt the betrayal of disobeying something I knew my mother would never have allowed, doing something wrong, but also the selfishness of allowing her to be worried and in fear that something tragic had happened to me. I wasn't walking with the Lord then or in church, but I knew better. Deep in my heart, I knew I was wrong. The inner alarm was going off, and I could not quiet it. Shame, guilt, and fear set in.

Needless to say, I got in big trouble when I got home. I don't exactly remember the consequence, but repetitive sin would eventually silence the inner conviction until I was truly converted. I would just deny the feelings associated with my sin and the betrayal against God, my parents, and others. I was in full-on pride for a long time as I sought to do what I wanted, regardless of what God said, my parents said, or anyone else. I was following my flesh and carnal desires, not realizing I was storing up wrath against the day of judgment. Not to mention, I was oblivious to the long-term danger I was in, naturally and spiritually.

I am not proud of this story, nor that though I was afraid of getting in trouble, I was not afraid of my mother. Because of that, I could disobey despite knowing there would be dire consequences. How often we do this with God! We test and tempt God, dishonoring His grace and mercy by habitual sin and outright rebellion. We give excuses such as:

- **I will repent later**
- **God knows my heart**
- **I'm just human**

Or we just bypass the conviction of the Holy Spirit altogether and fulfill the lust of the flesh. Pride deceives us into thinking we can just absorb the consequences of our sin. Scripture is clear:

> *For the wages of sin is death; but the gift of God is eternal life through Jesus Christ our Lord (Romans 6:23).*

> *Be not deceived; God is not mocked: for whatsoever a man soweth, that shall he also reap. For he that soweth to his flesh shall of the flesh reap corruption; but he that soweth to the Spirit shall of the Spirit reap life everlasting (Galatians 6:7-8).*

The Greek word for sin is *hamartano/hamartia*, meaning to miss the mark, to err. The mark is the Word of God, Jesus, and truth. Jesus is the standard, and to sin is to miss the mark. To understand sin, we must first acknowledge and understand that there is a holy standard: Jesus. He is holy because He is the expressed image of the True and Living

God, Whose very nature and Name are Holy. Sin is not just conduct and behaviors that are wrong by moral standards. To sin is to depart from the holy standard of righteousness and truth inherent in the nature of God. Think of sin as being "off" or "off the mark."

We were created in God's image and likeness, which represents Him. When we sinned, we traded a holy nature for a carnal nature and became bent toward wickedness. Many of us would not characterize ourselves as wicked, evil, or unrighteous. However, without the redeeming work of Christ and the power and grace of Holy Spirit, we are wicked. The word wicked means to be bent. It means our default nature is evil, wrong, sin, and carnality.

There are different types of sin:

- **Sin:** manifestation of the carnal nature and its fleshly/lustful appetites, including rebellion against God
- **Trespass:** actions or conduct that violate the ways of righteousness; can be intentional or unintentional (think walking on someone's grass)
- **Iniquity:** a propensity toward sin; sin nature given full vent characterized by unrepentance

The Word says:

> *Be not deceived, God is not mocked; whatsoever a man soweth, that he shall also reap (Galatians 6:7).*

There are those who outright mock God, thumbing their nose at Him, sticking their chest out, and believing that they can do what they want and don't have to answer to God or have hell to pay.

> *Yet they say, The Lord shall not see, Neither shall the God of Jacob regard it (Psalm 94: 7).*

How proud and deceived we can be at times to think "God doesn't see" our sin.

Repentance

> *From that time Jesus began to preach, and to say,*
> *"Repent: for the kingdom of heaven is at hand"*
> *(Matthew 4:1).*

The word 'repent' is broken down this way: re, meaning again or do over, and "pent" from the word 'pensive' meaning to think. It means to regret, change one's mind, and turn away from sin and back to God. Repentance is not merely saying "oops, sorry" but is characterized by:

- **Godly sorrow:** sincere brokenness and regret
- **Contrition:** humility and earnest desire to submit to correction
- **Brokenheartedness over sin:** feeling the weight and impact of actions and awareness of the impact
- **Change of heart:** recognizing the need to change and corresponding actions to turn away from the behavior and choose the Word.

Scriptures say to bring forth fruits consistent with repentance (Matthew 3:8 and Luke 3:8).This means there should be some inward change that manifests outward evidence that repentance has taken place in the heart. Then, confession, repentance, apology, and acknowledgment follow. It is common to sin and then confess that one repents, but repentance is not just a confession. It is the internal response in your heart to the conviction of Holy Spirit, your conscience, or your awareness of sin.

The fruit of the Spirit should be evident in those who have repented, not just from an incident of sin but also from a lifestyle of sin.

When we come to Jesus Christ, the first thing we do is repent. This is the acknowledgment that we are sinners and in need of salvation. When we first accept salvation, we should have an awareness of our sin nature and the need for redemption. Our condition before Jesus Christ is often one where we don't have godly sorrow or conviction about sin. Conviction comes from Holy Spirit. In our unregenerated state, we may feel "bad" or "guilty" when we sin, but godly sorrow leads to repentance because Holy Spirit convicts us.

The revelation of the price Jesus paid on the cross for our sins should also bring conviction and repentance. In God's Presence, the more we come into the knowledge of His Holiness, the more aware we become of our sinful condition. Understanding our need for a savior is predicated on our awareness of our depraved nature without Jesus.

> *Behold, I was shapen in iniquity; and in sin did my mother conceive me (Psalm 51:5).*

> *For ye were sometimes darkness, but now are ye light in the Lord: walk as children of light (Ephesians 5:8).*

Once we understand these foundational truths, we can receive the conviction of Holy Spirit; then we can repent. The Lord gave me a compelling example of what it looks like to enter His Presence with our sin nature. It is like showing up to the Royal Wedding in sweats, toting bologna sandwiches. As soon as you walk through the door, you become aware of how you showed up and that you have come dressed inappropriately.

What you have brought is "junk" compared to the exquisite offerings being served. You realize you can't stay in the same clothes, with the same offerings, and in the same mindset; you need to change. With God, however, if you come with humility and confess your condition before Him, He will exchange your attire for beautiful and exquisite apparel, and it's His holiness. He will cleanse you with the "washing of the water by His Word," and once He has, you will be as He is—holy and righteous.

Pride would deny the need to change, try to crash the

wedding dressed inappropriately, and likely get you expelled from the event because you refuse to repent.

Repentance requires awareness, acknowledgment, and a change of heart and actions. This is not just about sinning one time or making a mistake; it's about allowing Holy Spirit to bring conviction and responding by agreeing with Him. It starts at the heart. Refusing to repent is evidence of pride in one's life.

It is very serious because once Holy Spirit stops convicting, a person risks being turned over to a reprobate mind. This means they are left to continue in their sin until it brings forth the recompense of it. A reprobate mind is marked by iniquity, a propensity to sin without conscience. It is a bent toward wickedness without remorse. This is a perilous place because without repentance and acknowledging sin, one will go on sinning, and there is no more sacrifice for sins. Jesus Christ is it, and repentance is necessary for salvation. There is no other way.

Repentance is critical because sin separates us from God, Who Is Holy.

> *But your iniquities have separated between you and your God, and your sins have hid his face from you, that he will not hear (Isaiah 59:2).*

When that happens, it can result in rejection. Repentance and redemption give us access back into the good graces of God. When we sin, fellowship with God is broken. It is restored through the redemptive work of Christ, but repentance must happen first. The correct response is to confess the sin and allow the conviction of Holy Spirit to work in your heart to change your mind, your decisions, and consequently your actions.

When we fear the Lord and allow the work of Holy Spirit to transform us through the Word, we identify with Him through our love of righteousness, holiness, and what is good, and our hatred for sin, evil, wickedness, and unrighteousness. Repentance looks like godly sorrow, a change of mind, a change of heart, acknowledgment of sin, a desire to change, breaking agreement with the sin.

Prayer and Declaration:

Lord, I declare my need for You every day of my life and my dependence on You for all I need for life and godliness. I renounce pride and self-sufficiency, idolatry, and any other thing or person I look to in the place of you. Lord, help me to see any idols I have erected in my heart, given place to in my mind, or allowed to take up residence in my life. Reveal any hidden sin and cleanse me with the washing of the water by Your Word. (Proverbs 21:31; Psalm 24:3-4; Proverbs 16:18; 1 Corinthians 10:14; 1 John 5:21)

Chapter 10

The Carnal Mind

*And my speech and my preaching was not
with enticing words of man's wisdom, but in
demonstration of the Spirit and of power: That
your faith should not stand in the wisdom of
men but in the power of God.*

1 Corinthians 2:4-5

*But the natural man receiveth not the things
of the Spirit of God: for they are foolishness
unto him: neither can he know them, because
they are spiritually discerned. But he that is
spiritual judgeth all things, yet he himself is
judged of no man.*

1 Corinthians 2:14 –15

*For to be carnally minded is death; but to be
spiritually minded is life and peace. Because
the carnal mind is enmity against God: for it
is not subject to the law of God, neither indeed
can be. So then they that are in the flesh cannot
please God.*

Romans 8:6-8

These scriptures make a clear distinction between being
spiritual and being carnal and in the flesh. To be carnal is
to be in the flesh and is to mind the things of the flesh—the
lust of the flesh, the lust of the eyes, and the pride of life.
But the Lord says that to be carnally minded is death. The
result of following after the flesh is death. Carnal-minded
people cannot discern spiritual things because their focus
is the sensual. The mind that is carnal and focused on the
things of this world is enmity against God, hostile and

antagonistic toward Him. One cannot please God and be in the flesh; it is impossible.

> *So then they that are in the flesh cannot please God (Romans 8:8).*

The challenge for the believer is to walk in the spirit so that we won't fulfill the lust of the flesh. We often attempt to deal with our carnal nature by willing ourselves to "behave" or "do right." The key to dealing with a carnal mind is found in Romans 12:1-2:

> *I beseech you therefore, brethren, by the mercies of God, that ye present your bodies a living sacrifice, holy, and acceptable unto God, which is your reasonable service. And be not conformed to this world: but be ye transformed by the renewing of your mind, that ye may prove what is that good, and acceptable, and perfect, will of God.*

Walking in the spirit is our daily challenge as we allow the fear of the Lord to bring us into subjection to the Spirit.

We were created in the image and likeness of God. Jesus is our example, and He gave us Holy Spirit to empower us to live and reflect Christ. When we sin, we miss this mark. The "mark" we miss is the original design to reflect His glory, nature, and holiness in the earth. When Eve listened to the serpent, she opened humanity up to pride, flesh, and carnality. Until man is reconciled to God through Christ Jesus, he is ruled by this carnal/fleshly/sin nature, driven to fulfill the lusts and desires thereof, which is opposed to God.

> *All have sinned and fallen short of the glory of God (Romans 3:23).*

No one is exempt. Because we were born in sin and shaped in iniquity, our default setting is the flesh and our carnal nature. When we come to Christ, He resets us.

If any man be in Christ he is a new creature; old things are passed away; behold, all things are become new (2 Corinthians 5:17).

While sin manifests in the sum of our sin nature, its propensities and desires are the products of mindsets, heart conditions, decisions, and actions contrary to God. Sin is seen in the works of the flesh outlined in Galatians 5:19.

The works of the flesh manifest as:

- Adultery
- Fornication
- Uncleanness
- Lasciviousness
- Idolatry
- Witchcraft
- Hatred
- Variance
- Emulations
- Wrath
- Strife
- Seditions
- Heresies
- Envying
- Murders
- Drunkenness
- Reveling

Those who practice these works of the flesh will not inherit the kingdom of God. Galatians 5:22–23 contrasts them with the fruit of the Spirit. The fruit of the Spirit is:

- Love
- Joy
- Peace
- Longsuffering
- Gentleness
- Goodness
- Faith
- Meekness

- Temperance

The fruit of the Spirit is evidence of the grace and the power of Holy Spirit at work in the life of the believer.

So, what is the Kingdom of God? Righteousness, peace and joy in the Holy Ghost (Romans 14:17). It is the peace of knowing we are in right standing with God; we have His acceptance and approval, blessing, favor, provision, and protection. It also means we have His Holy Spirit to empower us to live righteously before Him so we don't sin and miss the "mark." We are then able to reflect His image and likeness.

This is not about an outward or physical likeness but His Holy, good, righteous, and just nature. We reflect His spiritual image that brings Him glory as He intended. The Kingdom of God is seen in the rule and reign of Truth by way of Jesus Christ, whereby we walk in the light or revelation of God and live accordingly.

What does this have to do with fear? As discussed previously, sin brings apprehension. It nags at our conscience to bring God's disapproval. The more we practice sin and allow pride and the flesh to override our conscience and Holy Spirit's conviction, the further into darkness and deception we go. This takes us away from the fear of the Lord to pride, idolatry, rebellion, and lawlessness. When we live in sin, we no longer carry the image and likeness of God, and we move further away from God's original plan and purpose for us. When we live lives of sin and rebellion, we look like Satan, the god of this world who has blinded the minds of unbelievers. (2 Corinthians 4:4)

Satan has been eternally rejected, and he uses seduction, lies, deception, and accusation to bring people into sin and condemnation. He uses the same methods today as he used in the garden with Eve. He:
- **Lies, he twists and deceives**
- **Seduces, entices, and suggests disobedience, rebellion, and sin**
- **Accuses**

Once we accept these, rejection and fear follow. Our greatest fear is to be rejected by God. This is condemnation.

Condemnation is a rendering of judgment against someone or something based on what is legally or morally required. It is often accompanied by the infliction of some form of punishment determined to be final without possibility of redemption. God condemned sin through Jesus Christ by His death on the cross. Condemnation is a type of final judgment and punishment. It represents a point of no return. God, in His holiness, condemns sin. His judgment of sin will not change because of His holy nature. Period.

Satan is a trafficker, merchandiser, and promoter of sin. He works in darkness and deception to bring humanity into sin and condemnation. If he can get humankind to follow our sin nature and fulfill the lust of the flesh, we will miss the plan of God for our lives. The goal is to get as many as possible into the same condemnation and rejection by God that he is in. Satan is beyond redemption. We are not; we have redemption through Jesus Christ. Satan, the enemy of our souls, seeks to deceive us into rejecting God and His plan for our lives and trade it for sin—the lust of the flesh, the lust of the eyes, and the pride of life. He has fashioned this world system in opposition to God and established it to have all the trappings of life suited to the flesh and carnal nature. It is a system based on lies, deception, counterfeits, and facades to give the illusion of "good." But the word tells us:

> *Love not the world, neither the things that are in the world. If any man love the world, the love of the Father is not in him. For all that is in the world, the lust of the flesh, and the lust of the eyes, and the pride of life, is not of the Father, but is of this world. And the world passeth away, and the lust thereof: but he that doeth the will of God abideth for ever (1 John 2:15-17).*

The world system is an anti-Christ system. It is a system of lies, confusion, and betrayal. Fear keeps the system going. Not the fear of the Lord but fear according to the natural. Fear of rejection, fear of not having enough, fear of sickness, and fear of death—things that the fear of the Lord would insulate us from.

The same way the serpent beguiled Eve by introducing the fear that God was keeping something from her is the same way he deceives today. By twisting God's motives in Eve's eyes, he was able to bring God's holy, good, and righteous character into question in Eve's mind. Satan lies because there is no truth in him. So, if Satan is speaking, no matter how correct or factual, he cannot speak truth because his whole nature is to lie. Anything put forth by Satan that has any truth is turned into a lie because he has no truth in him.

Prayer:
Thank You, Lord, for the life and peace that comes with a spiritual mind. I walk in the spirit and will not fulfill the lusts of the flesh that come from acting on carnal thoughts. Lord, Your Word says I can't please You in the flesh, so I set my heart to walk in the spirit daily (Romans 8:6-8; Galatians 5:16-26).

Chapter 11

The Gall of Bitterness and an Evil Heart of Unbelief

Lest there should be any among you, man or woman, or family, or tribe, whose heart turneth away this day from the Lord our God, to go and serve other gods of these nations, lest there should be among you a root that beareth gall and wormwood.

Deuteronomy 29:18

Gall and wormwood are poisonous water.

Looking diligently lest any man fail of the grace of God, lest any root of bitterness springing up trouble you and hereby many be defiled; (Hebrews 12:15)

The nation of Israel was warned about individuals among the tribe who, through their hard hearts, rebelliousness toward God with an evil heart of unbelief, and callousness and complacency, would cause a bitter root to spring up, infecting the whole camp.

Bitterness is often associated with allowing offense to fester in our hearts, turning to bitterness. The warning here is speaking of something altogether different. The context in which Deuteronomy 29:18 and Hebrews 12:15 are stated has to do with those within the tribe who, through their iniquity, would begin to poison others so that they cause them to depart from faith in the true and living God.

Simon the Sorcerer is the example.

And when Simon saw that through laying on of

the apostle's hands, the Holy Ghost was given, he offered them money, Saying give me also this power, that on whomsoever I lay hands, he may receive the Holy Ghost. But Peter said unto him, Thy money perish with thee because thou has thought that the gift of God may be purchased with money. Thou has neither part nor lot in this matter: <u>for thy heart is not right in the sight of God</u>. Repent therefore of this wickedness and pray God if perhaps the thought of thine heart may be forgiven thee. For I perceive <u>that thou art in the gall of bitterness</u>, and in the bond of iniquity (Acts 8:18-23 emphasis added).

Wherefore as the Holy Ghost saith, to day if ye will hear his voice, <u>Harden not your hearts</u>, as in the provocation, in the day of temptation in the wilderness when your fathers tempted and proved me, and saw my works forty years. Wherefore I was grieved with that generation, and said, <u>they do always err in their hearts: and they have not known my ways</u>. So I sware in my wrath, they shall not enter into my rest. Take heed, brethren, lest there be in any of you <u>an evil heart of unbelief in departing from the living God</u> (Hebrews 3:8-12 emphasis added).

These scriptures describe a condition of the heart, characterized by a lack of fear of the Lord—iniquity, hard heart, having no knowledge of God nor regarding Him. This person is ripe to become a source of poison and corruption to others.

The words used for poison are *gall*, meaning hemlock or venom, and *wormwood*, which means to poison or to curse *(la anah)*. Poison makes things bitter and unfit for consumption. A root of bitterness represents the one among the congregation who poisons the group.

An Evil Heart of Unbelief

For as many as are led by the Spirit of God, they are the sons of God. For ye have not received the spirit of bondage again to fear, but ye have received the Spirit of adoption, whereby we cry Abba, Father (Romans 8:14-15).

Take heed, brethren, lest there be in any of you an evil heart of unbelief, in departing from the living God (Hebrews 3:12).

And to whom sware he that they should not enter into his rest, <u>but to them that believed not.</u> So we see that <u>they could not enter in because of unbelief</u> (Hebrews 3: 19 emphasis added).

Unless we believe, as evidenced by our faith and obedience, we will not enter God's rest. When we don't believe, we fear; when we fear, we can't rest. If we constantly question God's faithfulness, His Word, and His power, if we believe the enemy and follow what he is saying and reject what God has proclaimed, we open the door to the wrong kind of fear—the fear of His wrath, fear of evil, etc.

Unbelief manifests in denying God's power. It is a lack of reverential fear and acknowledgment of Him. Many people claim to follow God, but their lives reveal unbelief. They don't live in reverence to God, though they may say they believe He exists. This is a grave error and deception because when we fail to acknowledge God and reverence Him, we can set ourselves up for judgment and eternal separation from Him.

We must check our hearts and examine our ways, walking circumspectly before God to ensure that we are not in the gall of bitterness and have an evil heart of unbelief. The Bible calls it an evil heart. This suggests that this is not just mere error but that it is out of iniquity, which is not just sinful actions but a heart bent toward sin.

But without faith it is impossible to please him:
for he that cometh to God must believe that he is,
and that he is a rewarder of them that diligently
seek him (Hebrews 11:6).

If we come to God, we must be fully persuaded and con-
vinced of His existence, that He is real and living, and that
if we seek Him, He will reveal Himself to us and answer us.

God does have standards and commandments. He is
Holy. But because He empowers us, He can expect us to
fulfill them because He works in us to will and to do His
good pleasure (Philippians 2:13).

But we must believe and have faith.

Jesus tells all who are weighed down by the heaviness of
sin to come to Him; He promises to give us rest. His yoke
is easy, and His burden is light (Matthew 11:30). But we are
admonished to be careful not to depart from God through
the deceitfulness of sin and be found to have an evil heart
of unbelief. There is no rest for the one whose heart is hard.
A hard heart rejects God.

Good understanding giveth favour but the way of
the transgressor is hard (Proverbs 13:15).

God said He would take out our stony hearts and put in a
heart of flesh (one that is tender toward the things of God)
that we would keep His commandments, that He would be
our God, and we would be His people (Ezekiel 36: 26-28).

The Old Covenant revealed His commandments and
a system of sacrifice and offerings to atone for sin. In the
New Covenant, Jesus is that sacrifice, but He died once and
for all and gave Holy Spirit to empower us to live holy and
righteous before God.

Lack of faith is evidence of the presence of fear. Faith is
trust and love to God, and it produces reverential fear. Fear
and apprehension result when we don't have faith and trust
in God. Then, everything we do is out of fear. We can also
fall into the error of rejecting God because we are afraid

of Him. Again, our fear of God is to be reverential, where we have a revelation of His good and Holy Nature and not based on the false notion that He rejects us.

Prayer:

Lord, search my heart and see if there be any wicked way in me. Father, I lay my heart bare before You that You would reveal all wrong motives or evil motives of my heart. I ask You to create in me a clean heart and renew a right spirit in me so that I may walk in the fear of the Lord. I receive a heart of faith whereby I will please you (Psalm 139:23-24; Jeremiah 17:9-10; Hebrews 11:6; Psalm 51:10).

Chapter 12

Bitterness, Unforgiveness and Fear

*A brother offended is harder to be won
than a defensed city.*

Proverbs 18:19

Satan uses offense as a trap to foster division and bring acrimony among believers and others. When someone offends us, we have a choice: we can forgive and work toward resolution or reconciliation where possible, or we can take the offense, hold it in our hearts, and allow it to fester. When we fail or refuse to forgive, we open the door to unforgiveness.

As followers of Christ, we are warned that offenses will come but not to take them. Christ made it clear that there will be occasions to be offended and hurt by the actions or words of others, but we must forgive as God has forgiven us. If we don't forgive our brother or sister, then God cannot forgive us. Holy Spirit gives us the grace to do what God requires of us.

Deep hurts can be difficult to overcome and create fear of entering relationships to avoid further hurt and offense. However, we must allow Holy Spirit to work in us to will and to do what pleases God, and that's forgiveness. God is able to help us heal from the hurts that we experience. Forgiveness is a decision, but healing from hurt takes time. The Lord knows our frame and is patient and merciful if we are willing and obedient to forgive. No offense is exempt from forgiveness.

The Greek word for offense is *skandalon*, from which we get the word 'scandal.' It is commonly associated with a sensational conflict involving a sordid controversy between individuals. The meaning of *skandalon* is an occasion to fall, a stumbling block, cause of displeasure or sin, a thing that offends, cause of offense and indignation.

There are many opportunities throughout life to be offended or take offense at the actions of others. Some are minor, and others can be traumatic.

God knew that we would experience these things due to man's fall, but He is able to heal through and through. We must be willing to forgive. We cannot allow the offense of another to keep us from our eternal reward. Nothing is worth our relationship with the Lord. In addition, to hold unforgiveness against another only hurts you. It has been described as taking poison, hoping the other person will die.

Unforgiveness is characterized by bitterness, where a person has held so long to the offense that it has caused them to internalize it and hold anger, resentment, and even hatred in their heart. This is a dangerous place as it puts a person at odds with God because He requires us to forgive. It is also a form of pride and idolatry to put one's offense ahead of the Word and will of God. What has happened to many can be a source of extremely deep pain that can be difficult to get over. However, Holy Spirit is our Comforter and Spirit of Grace—He can strengthen, encourage, and restore us. Given this, we have no excuse. All we need to do is agree with God and forgive. When we fear the Lord, we don't obey His Word based on our feelings. We simply agree with His Word and surrender to His process so He can cleanse, heal, and restore us. We need not fear trusting others or having "trust issues" because we are not to put our trust in man.

When we harbor offense, we enter relationships with a mindset of self-preservation. So, we protect ourselves from further hurt, pain, and betrayal by betraying others. The fear of being hurt again drives how we interact in relationships if we fail to deal with offense. We often expend a lot of energy trying to prevent being betrayed and hurt that we can't see clearly and can't function appropriately in relationships. Unforgiveness can lead to:

- **Distrust:** not trusting people, even those who mean no harm

- **Mistrust:** trusting the wrong people because of a distorted view
- **Suspicion:** creating scenarios of hurt and betrayal rooted in fear with no basis in fact or truth
- **Hard heart:** You are no longer sensitive to the voice of God, and the Word and Holy Spirit can't break through with truth
- **Darkened heart:** Falling into deception, rejecting the promptings of Holy Spirit to repent and forgive, deceived into thinking that one is justified in their offense, refusing to forgive. Also, having no conviction about holding offense or operating in unforgiveness.

Those who allow offense to lead to fear:
- **Commit acts of treason:** become disloyal and look out for their own interests at the expense of the community
- **Become traitors:** Sell out to the enemy
- **Disloyal:** Can't be trusted to consider the other person's interests
- **Hypocrisy:** Demands loyalty but violates commitment and loyalty themselves
- **Compromise:** Will act against what they know is right to suit their needs or protect their own interests

When we don't fear the Lord, we will default to the fear of man. This can lead to idolatry, men-pleasing, seeking affirmation from man, and loss of identity and sonship. We cannot allow fear of men's disapproval nor fear of rejection to cause us to disobey God, sin, or engage in ungodly behavior.

Fear of man is an affront to God because it is idolatry. In addition, if we are so guarded that we distrust and mistrust people, how can we fulfill God's call to minister to people? We are *all* called to minister to people, which requires rapport and relationship. If we allow our offenses and unforgiveness against people to keep us from engaging them out of fear, we will never be used by God. This is a place to repent and seek the Lord for healing and deliverance. Search the scriptures for God's Word and renew your mind so that the fear of the Lord is restored to your heart.

Many years ago, the Lord exposed unforgiveness in my heart toward my sister. I had held on to some unresolved issues that I had allowed to build up, and I didn't realize that it was unforgiveness. It began to manifest as a critical spirit, passive aggression, and resentment. Soon, the Lord would release the tormentors. I had no peace or rest until I repented and talked through the issues. Once I did, we were able to reconcile the issue, and my peace returned to me.

The Lord taught me through His Word that I cannot hold unforgiveness against others and expect Him to forgive my sins. Matthew 18:21–35 tells of the parable of the unforgiving servant and reveals the consequences of having our debts forgiven and turning around and holding another's debts to us against them. The torment is a real thing. The Lord will surely deal with you, and you will not have peace until you repent, forgive, and release those who have wronged you.

> Then Peter came up and said to him, "Lord, how often will my brother sin against me, and I forgive him? As many as seven times?" Jesus said to him, "I do not say to you seven times, but seventy-seven times (Matthew 18:21,22).
>
> Therefore the kingdom of heaven may be compared to a king who wished to settle accounts with his servants. When he began to settle, one was brought to him who owed him ten thousand talents. And since he could not pay, his master ordered him to be sold, with his wife and children and all that he had, and payment to be made. So the servant fell on his knees, imploring him, 'Have patience with me, and I will pay you everything.' And out of pity for him, the master of that servant released him and forgave him the debt. But when

that same servant went out, he found one of his fellow servants who owed him a hundred denarii, and seizing him, he began to choke him, saying, 'Pay what you owe.' So his fellow servant fell down and pleaded with him, 'Have patience with me, and I will pay you.' He refused and went and put him in prison until he should pay the debt. When his fellow servants saw what had taken place, they were greatly distressed, and they went and reported to their master all that had taken place. Then his master summoned him and said to him, 'You wicked servant! I forgave you all that debt because you pleaded with me. And should not you have had mercy on your fellow servant, as I had mercy on you?' And in anger his master delivered him to the jailers, until he should pay all his debt. So also my heavenly Father will do to every one of you, if you do not forgive your brother from your heart"(Matthew 18:23-35 ESV).

Prayer:

Lord, help me to walk in forgiveness continually and not allow offense to fester in my life. Just as you forgave me, I will forgive others. I will love my enemies, bless those who curse me, do good to those who hate me, and pray for those who persecute me and despitefully use me. In this, I will be a reflection of Your love, mercy, and forgiveness. I will not fear being hurt by man, but will forgive as many times as I have occasion to be offended. (Matthew 5:43-48; Matthew 18:21-22)

Chapter 13

Spirit of Bondage and Slavery, Orphan vs. Sonship

For as many as are led by the Spirit of God, they are the sons of God. For ye have not received the spirit of bondage again to fear; but ye have received the Spirit of adoption, whereby we cry, Abba, Father. The Spirit itself beareth witness with our spirit, that we are the children of God: And if children, then heirs; heirs of God, and joint-heirs with Christ; if so be that we suffer with him, that we may be also glorified together.

Romans 8:14-17

For all who are led by the Spirit of God are children of God. So you have not received a spirit that makes you fearful slaves. Instead, you received God's Spirit when he adopted you as his own children. Now we call him, "Abba, Father." For his Spirit joins with our spirit to affirm that we are God's children. And since we are his children, we are his heirs. In fact, together with Christ we are heirs of God's glory. But if we are to share his glory, we must also share his suffering.

Romans 8:14 NLT

In our pursuit of God, many of us have sadly found ourselves in situations, systems, and institutions of religion that produce a slave mentality. Many of the religious organizations today are borne out of the world system. They are often large organizations, networks, and systems designed to perpetuate religious practice void of true relationship with God. Not all, but many. Many do not emphasize relationship with God through Jesus Christ but through rules, rituals, and works toward salvation.

The Church—the *Ekklesia*—is a people, the Body of Christ, a living organism. God's plan is to restore to Himself a bride prepared for His coming. As the Church, a body, a people, God works through us by Holy Spirit, empowering us to live holy and righteous lives that reflect His nature. Spirits of bondage and religious spirits bind us to attempt to produce righteousness by following rules, laws, and rituals and doing outward things to obtain right standing with God.

> *Wherefore the law was our schoolmaster to bring us unto Christ, that we might be justified by faith. But after that faith is come, we are no longer under a schoolmaster. For ye are all the children of God by faith in Christ Jesus (Galatians 3:24-26).*

Faith in Jesus is evidenced by our lives being transformed into His image. It is what makes us His children, His off-spring. Our righteousness comes from faith in Christ and by the power of Holy Spirit to live righteous. We cannot keep the law in our flesh. It is impossible because of the corrupt nature of the flesh.

> *O foolish Galatians, who hath bewitched you, that ye should not obey the truth, before whose eyes Jesus Christ hath been evidently set forth, crucified among you? This only would I learn of you. Received ye the Spirit by the works of the law, or by the hearing of faith? Are ye so foolish? Having begun in the Spirit, are ye now made perfect by the flesh? (Galatians 3:1-3).*

The Jews, at Peter's leading, were attempting to get the Gentile converts to keep the law to be accepted. All the ordinances and rituals were a shadow of things to come and would point them to Jesus Christ. They were a school-master. The law in the sight of God justifies no one. This is because no one can keep the law. Cursed is everyone who does not continue in all the things written in the law book to do them. Christ redeemed us by becoming a curse for us. Spirits of bondage keep us bound to the works of the law. The law in and of itself is not bad, but the law does not have the effect of making us righteous.

> *For it is not possible that the blood of bulls and of goats should take away sins (Hebrews 10:4).*

The spirit of bondage is woven into the religious system by producing fear of rejection by God and fear of condemnation for failure to comply with rules and rituals that often have nothing to do with God.

> *Howbeit in vain do they worship me teaching for doctrines the commandments of men, For laying aside the commandments of God, ye hold the tradition of men, as the washing of pots and cups: and many other such things ye do. And he said to them, Full well ye reject the commandment of God, that ye may keep your own tradition (Mark 7:7-9).*

> *Making the word of God of none effect through your tradition, which ye have delivered: and many such like things do ye (Mark 7:13).*

Many religious institutions perpetuate fear by teaching traditions, rules, and requirements of men as if they are commandments of God and then use fear—fear of pun-ishment, rejection, and condemnation— to keep people in bondage. There is a form of godliness but a denial of power. These are man-made rules and requirements with no power to live or walk them out.

> *For they bind heavy burdens and grievous to be*
> *borne and lay them on men's shoulders; but they*
> *themselves will not move them with one of their*
> *fingers (Matthew 23:4).*

They don't follow them but expect those under them to follow them. The threat of punishment or rejection by God becomes a means to control and bind people. This is a clear tactic of the enemy and must be discerned and rejected. When we attempt to be saved by keeping man-made laws and rules, we inevitably find ourselves in bondage, which God never intended. God never intended for man to control or dominate another person—even through rules.

The life we live is a life of freedom by Holy Spirit and is the life of Jesus Christ, His Holy nature lived and walked out through us. It is the life Jesus died to give us so we would be free to live righteously. We can comply with rules, but that, in and of itself, does not make us righteous. We need the power of Holy Spirit to give us the grace to walk out righteousness. Christ redeemed us and blotted out the ordinances or the legal debt against us by dying on the cross. It is our faith that gives us right standing with God.

> *Blotting out the handwriting of ordinances that*
> *was against us which was contrary to us. And he*
> *has taken it out of the way, nailing it to his cross;*
> *And having spoiled principalities and powers, he*
> *made a shew of them openly, triumphing over*
> *them in it. Let no man therefore judge you in*
> *meat, or drink, or in respect of an holyday, or*
> *the new moon, or of the sabbath days: which are*
> *a shadow of things to come; but the body is of*
> *Christ (Colossians 2:14).*

Now, we have received the spirit of adoption where we experience and know God as Father and are received as His sons. We don't have the sense of apprehension and fear from not keeping the law, but we now live out our lives in devotion to God out of relationship, not as slaves. We are sons (and daughters) of God, not slaves to a system and institution of man-made religious rules disguised as requirements to appease an angry God. He is our Father, and we are His beloved, so the fear that He produces is in us a reverential, not terror.

The Church—the *Ekklesia*—is Christ's glorious Bride, and God loves her. She is not a building, denomination, or organization but the Body of Christ. Though God ordains and uses buildings and organizations and has standards and order, it is divinely inspired by Him, not man-made.

Prayer:
Lord, You have not given me a spirit that binds me to laws, rules, and rituals that if I don't do them, I am disqualified from belonging to You. But I thank You that You have given me the Spirit of adoption that makes me a son, so I enjoy the benefits of sonship based on relationship. I can come to You as my Heavenly Father and address You in terms of endearment because I am Yours. I declare that I have a Father in Heaven; I am not an orphan or slave but a son. I follow Your Word out of love and devotion to You, NOT out of obligation or fear of Your anger (Romans 8:15).

Chapter 14

Identity

For I reckon that the sufferings of this present time are not worthy to be compared with the glory which shall be revealed in us. For the earnest expectation of the creature waiteth for the manifestation of the sons of God.

Romans 8:18,19

Who are you? Who am I? The answers to these questions and others about our identity, our purpose, and God's plan for our lives are found in Him. We are all born to natural parents, but our identity comes from God. He is our Creator. This is what Scripture reveals about who we are:

- **He created us in His image and likeness (Genesis 1:27)**
- **Before He formed us in our mother's womb, He knew us (Jeremiah 1:5)**
- **We are fearfully and wonderfully made (Psalm 139:14)**
- **In His Book, all our members were written (Psalm 139:16)**

God foreknew us, and we are His Creation. Our identity is rooted and grounded in who God says we are. He says:

- **We are sons(daughters): Son as in offspring, not just the gender-specific (Galatians 3:26)**
- **We are accepted in the Beloved (Ephesians 1:6)**
- **Nothing can separate us from His love for us that is in Christ Jesus (Romans 8:38–39)**
- **We are His workmanship (Ephesians 2:10)**
- **We are Kings and Priests (Revelation 1:6)**
- **More than conquerors (Romans 8:37)**

- Strong in the power of His might (Ephesians 6:10)
- Partakers of His divine nature (2 Peter 1:4)
- We are joint heirs with Christ (Romans 8:17)
- We are the righteousness of God in Christ Jesus (2 Corinthians 5:21)

The most important part of our identity is that of sons and daughters. We are God's children, and God is our Heavenly Father. We who received Him have the spirit of adoption; He is our "Abba Father." This is the same as the term of endearment, "Papa" or "Daddy," reserved for familial father/child relationships. That is Who He Is to us.

The revelation of Who God Is as Father is a key part of our redemption. The whole point of Jesus dying on the cross for our sins was to restore us back to God so that we would enjoy fellowship, sonship, and relationship with God. When sin no longer separates us, we can approach God boldly; we can represent Him as sons and daughters and be His representative agents in the earth to draw others back to Him. Jesus died for us as an expression of God's love for us. The fear of the Lord should bring us into greater revelation and discovery of who we are. We identify with Him.

For very long in my life, I had come to identify with what I did. I got validation of who I was not from my identity in God but from my job titles, positions, and even my achievements or lack thereof. It would take the Lord to disavow me of the notion that my identity was in what I was hired to do or what position I held in the marketplace. It was painful to have to have these stripped away, only to realize that they were not who I was.

My journey to sonship and learning God as my Father and my identity in Christ caused me to turn a corner in my walk with Him. I would come to let go of trying to be something I wasn't or who God didn't create me to be, and I would discover who He created me to be and embrace it. This changed my life and I'm still walking in this glorious revelation and am enjoying walking in my identity in Christ.

We are called by His Name

I will say to the north, give up; and to the south, keep not back: bring my sons from far, and my daughters from the ends of the earth; even every one that is called by my name: for I have created him for my glory, I have formed him; yea, I have made him (Isaiah 43:6-7).

If my people, which are called by my name, shall humble themselves, and pray, and seek my face, and turn from their wicked ways; then will I hear from heaven, and will forgive their sin, and will heal their land (2 Chronicles 7:14).

What does it mean to be called by God's Name? To be called by His Name is to be identified with Him. We are His people; we share His identity, spiritual lineage, heritage, and DNA. We were created in His image and likeness, and we have His divine nature. Because we have His Holy Spirit, we have His power and His grace to reflect His glory.

He works in us to will and to do His good pleasure (Philippians 2:13).

So, what does this all mean? It means we live to glorify Him. We live to represent Him in the earth. We don't seek our identity outside of His sovereign will, design, and purpose for our lives. Rather, we seek to discover who we are by seeking Him as He reveals His divine plan for His creation. God reveals Himself to us. We then seek to know Him by seeking Him through prayer, His Word—the Bible—worship, and time spent in devotion to Him.

Our life's journey is to know Him and fulfill the plan and purpose for which He has created us. Before we came to Christ and were reconciled to God, we likely took on an identity shaped by the world's standards. You likely have even believed you should look, act, and think in ways that were not in alignment with who you were created to be. Sin, trauma, and the darkness of this world have effectively kept us from knowing who we are in God—our true identity.

What's in a Name?

What you are called matters, who named you matters. Historically, fathers gave their children their identity through their names. Names had meaning, and even family names were instrumental in shaping identity and destiny. Fathers, in giving their children names, had the power to speak over and into their children's lives. They would then grow up with a clear sense of identity and purpose, knowing who they are. A child's experience with their natural father can shape how they view God as Heavenly Father.

Absent fathers can lead a child to fear, rejection, and abandonment and lead to an orphan spirit viewing God from the mindset of an orphan. This makes it very difficult to have the fear of the Lord in a reverential way. What should be reverential fear—honor and respect for the Lord—can instead be fear of rejection and abandonment, feeling unaccepted, unloved, and unprotected by God as Father.

When we remember Who God Is, we can rest assured that He is Who He says He Is.

- **He is Holy**
- **He is good**
- **He is faithful**
- **He is True**
-

Nothing can separate us from His love that is in Christ Jesus (Romans 8:31–39).

He created us for Himself and so loved us that He sent His only Son to die on the cross for our sins so we could be reconciled to Him. No matter our experience with our natural fathers, God is a good, faithful Father. He is not like man; there is no shadow of turning with God, and we love Him because He first loved us (1 John 4:19).

We discover our identity in Him by seeking Him, spending time in His presence, and journeying through life with

Him. As He reveals Who He Is, we not only know who we are, but our identity in Him unfolds, and we become who He created us to be. This is the wonderful part of the fear of the Lord—it leads us to honor Him and the life He so graciously gave us. We are redeemed so that we may enjoy the benefits of sonship and fellowship with Him eternally.

Declaration:
I declare that I am a son of God, made in His Image and likeness, and I am conformed to the image of Christ. My identity is in Him as a child of God first and foremost. I embrace who You say I am and who You created me to be. I will live my life to bring glory to You. (Genesis 1:27; Psalm 139:14)

Chapter 15

Perfect Love Casts Out Fear

Beloved, let us love one another: for love is of God, and everyone that loveth is born of God and knoweth God.

He that loveth not, knoweth not God, for God is love.

In this was manifested the love of God toward us because that God sent his only begotten Son into the world, that we might love through him. Therein is love, not that we loved God, but that He loved us, and sent his son to be the propitiation for our sins

Beloved, if God so loved us, we ought also love one another.

No man hath seen God at any time. If we love one another, God dwelleth in us, and his love is perfected in us.

Whosoever shall confess that Jesus is the Son of God, God dwelleth in him, and he in God. And we have known and believed the love that God hath to us. God is love; and he that dwelleth in love dwelleth in God and God in him. Herein is our love made perfect, that we have boldness in the day of judgment because as he is, so are we in this world.

There is no fear in love, but perfect love casteth out fear, because fear hath torment.

He that feareth is not made perfect in love. We love him because He first loved us.

1 John 4:7-19

The answer to ungodly fear is the revelation of God's love. We have to believe God loves us and stand in faith on that truth against all that comes to try to get us to think and believe God does not love us and against every distortion of the truth. We must not let anyone or anything get in the way of our faith and belief in God's love for us.

> *Who shall separate us from the love of Christ? Shall tribulation, or distress, or persecution, or famine, or nakedness, or peril, or sword? (Romans 8:35).*

> *For I am fully persuaded, that neither death, nor life, nor angels, nor principalities, nor powers, nor things present, nor things to come, nor height, nor depth, nor any other creature shall be able to separate us from the love of God, which is in Christ Jesus our Lord (Romans 8:38-39).*

Ungodly fear is rooted in not knowing or having a revelation of God's love toward us. When we receive God's love, we love as He loves. We become extensions of His love. This is what it means to be perfected in love. It is to have love come to fruition and maturity, full-grown and fully manifested— its fullest expression. As God, Who is love, is, so are we in this world.

1 John 4:18 tells us there is no fear in love; when love is perfected in us, we have no reason to fear. There is no sense of apprehension, foreboding, timidity, or uncertainty about our standing with God when we know God's love for us, accept it, and believe it. This is why Romans 8:35-38 stands as an encouragement to us—Nothing shall separate us *from the love of God, which is in Christ Jesus.*

We are fully persuaded, and nothing can cause us to doubt, have unbelief, or convince us otherwise. The Love of God toward us is in His Son, whom He gave to reconcile us to Him. It was all out of His love.

We are tormented when we allow fear, reject, or doubt

God's love. We often end up rejected and in a cycle of fear and apprehension, going to and from, trying to protect ourselves, covering ourselves with fig leaves, and never believing we are loved and accepted by God. We have no rest. This is not God's plan or will for us. Instead, we can abide in the reverential fear of the Lord rooted in our love and devotion toward Him.

> *Who (God our Savior) will have all men to be saved, and to come unto the knowledge of the truth. For there is one God, and one Mediator between God and men, the man Christ Jesus, Who gave himself a ransom for all, to be testified in due time (1 Timothy 2:4-5).*

> *Then said Jesus to those Jews which believed on him, If ye continue in my word, then ye are my disciples indeed; And ye shall know the truth and the truth shall make you free (John 8:31-32).*

> *Jesus said unto them, If God were your Father, ye would love me: for I proceeded forth and came from God; neither came I of myself, but he sent me (John 8:42).*

> *He that is of God heareth God's words: ye therefore hear them not because ye are not of God (John 8:47).*

The love of God that is God manifest in us toward Him, because of Him, and toward others casts out fear. It dismantles and does away with ungodly fear of God and the terror, torment, and fear of His wrath. We recognize that His wrath is set upon evil and that it is out of His love, holiness, righteousness, and justice that He judges sin. When we accept the love of God and believe, we manifest love and devotion to Him, and it causes us to have a desire to please Him and forsake sin. We desire to love holiness, righteousness, truth, and justice. We hate what He hates and love what He loves.

Without faith, it is impossible to please God.

> *Love not the world, neither the things that are in the world. If any man love the world, the love of the Father is not in him. For all that is in the world, the lust of the flesh, and the lust of the eyes, and the pride of life, is not of the Father but is of the world. And the world passeth away, and the lust thereof;* <u>*but he that doeth the will of God abideth forever*</u> *(1 John 2:15-17 emphasis added).*

Declaration:

I declare that I have a revelation of God's love toward me, and fear has no place in me. Because I know Your Love toward me, I am not fearful of Your wrath, evil, or any other thing; I have boldness in the day of judgment. (1 John 4:7-19)

Behold! The Fear of the Lord Scriptures

Exodus 14:31
And Israel saw that great work which the LORD did upon the Egyptians: and the people feared the LORD, and believed the LORD, and his servant Moses.

Leviticus 25:17
Ye shall not therefore oppress one another; but thou shalt fear thy God: for I am the LORD your God.

Deuteronomy 6:13
Thou shalt fear the LORD thy God, and serve him, and shalt swear by his name.

Joshua 22:25
For the LORD hath made Jordan a border between us and you, ye children of Reuben and children of Gad; ye have no part in the LORD: so shall your children make our children cease from fearing the LORD.

Job 1:9
Then Satan answered the LORD, and said, Doth Job fear God for nought?

Psalm 19:9
The fear of the LORD is clean, enduring for ever: the judgments of the LORD are true and righteous altogether.

Psalm 25:12
What man is he that feareth the LORD? him shall he teach in the way that he shall choose.

Proverbs 1:7
The fear of the LORD is the beginning of knowledge: but fools despise wisdom and instruction.

Proverbs 14:16
A wise man feareth, and departeth from evil: but the fool rageth, and is confident.

Ecclesiastes 12:13
Let us hear the conclusion of the whole matter: Fear God, and keep his commandments: for this is the whole duty of man.

Isaiah 59:19
So shall they fear the name of the LORD from the west, and his glory from the rising of the sun. When the enemy shall come in like a flood, the Spirit of the LORD shall lift up a standard against him.

Jeremiah 5:24
Neither say they in their heart, Let us now fear the LORD our God, that giveth rain, both the former and the latter, in his season: he reserveth unto us the appointed weeks of the harvest.

Nehemiah 5:15
But the former governors that had been before me were chargeable unto the people, and had taken of them bread and wine, beside forty shekels of silver; yea, even their servants bare rule over the people: but so did not I, because of the fear of God.

Proverbs 9:10
The fear of the LORD is the beginning of wisdom: and the knowledge of the holy is understanding.

Proverbs 10:27
The fear of the LORD prolongeth days: but the years of the wicked shall be shortened.

Psalm 25:14
The secret of the LORD is with them that fear him; and he will shew them his covenant.

Proverbs 8:13
The fear of the LORD is to hate evil: pride, and arrogancy, and the evil way, and the froward mouth, do I hate.

Isaiah 11:2
And the spirit of the LORD shall rest upon him, the spirit of wisdom and understanding, the spirit of counsel and might, the spirit of knowledge and of the fear of the LORD;

Isaiah 11:3
And shall make him of quick understanding in the fear of the LORD: and he shall not judge after the sight of his eyes, neither reprove after the hearing of his ears.

Deuteronomy 14:23
And thou shalt eat before the LORD thy God, in the place which he shall choose to place his name there, the tithe of thy corn, of thy wine, and of thine oil, and the firstlings of thy herds and of thy flocks; that thou mayest learn to fear the LORD thy God always.

2 Chronicles 20:29
And the fear of God was on all the kingdoms of those countries, when they had heard that the LORD fought against the enemies of Israel.

1Samuel 12:14
If ye will fear the LORD, and serve him, and obey his voice, and not rebel against the commandment of the LORD,

then shall both ye and also the king that reigneth over you continue following the LORD your God:

1 Samuel 11:7
And he took a yoke of oxen, and hewed them in pieces, and sent them throughout all the coasts of Israel by the hands of messengers, saying, Whosoever cometh not forth after Saul and after Samuel, so shall it be done unto his oxen. And the fear of the LORD fell on the people, and they came out with one consent.

Joshua 24:14
Now therefore fear the LORD, and serve him in sincerity and in truth: and put away the gods which your fathers served on the other side of the flood, and in Egypt; and serve ye the LORD.

Isaiah 50:10
Who is among you that feareth the LORD, that obeyeth the voice of his servant, that walketh in darkness, and hath no light? let him trust in the name of the LORD, and stay upon his God.

Jeremiah 5:22
Fear ye not me? saith the LORD: will ye not tremble at my presence, which have placed the sand for the bound of the sea by a perpetual decree, that it cannot pass it: and though the waves thereof toss themselves, yet can they not prevail; though they roar, yet can they not pass over it?

Deuteronomy 10:12
And now, Israel, what doth the LORD thy God require of thee, but to fear the LORD thy God, to walk in all his ways, and to love him, and to serve the LORD thy God with all thy heart and with all thy soul,

Exodus 1:17
But the midwives feared God, and did not as the king of Egypt commanded them, but saved the men children alive.

Daniel 6:26
I make a decree, That in every dominion of my kingdom men tremble and fear before the God of Daniel: for he is the living God, and stedfast for ever, and his kingdom that which shall not be destroyed, and his dominion shall be even unto the end.

Luke 23:40
But the other answering rebuked him, saying, Dost not thou fear God, seeing thou art in the same condemnation?

Acts 9:31
Then had the churches rest throughout all Judaea and Galilee and Samaria, and were edified; and walking in the fear of the Lord, and in the comfort of the Holy Ghost, were multiplied.

Acts 13:26
Men and brethren, children of the stock of Abraham, and whosoever among you feareth God, to you is the word of this salvation sent.

Works Cited

AMG Annotated Strong's Hebrew Dictionary of the Old Testament, Hebrew-Greek Keyword Study Bible, King James Version, 2nd Revised Edition. AMG International Inc. Publishers, Chattanooga, TN, 1984, 1990, 2008.

https://biblehub.com/topical/s/severity.htm. 2021

Cornerstone Encyclopedia of Bible Knowledge. Cornerstone Bible Publishers, Nashville TN, 2001)

Hebrew-Greek Keyword Study Bible, King James Version, 2nd Revised Edition. AMG International Inc. Publishers, Chattanooga, TN, 1984, 1990, 2008. p.1951.

Hemingway, Ernest. A Farewell to Arms. Scribner Classics, New York, NY, 1997

Master Study Bible. Cornerstone Bible Publishers, Nashville, TN, 2001, B-356-357.

Tozer, A.W. Knowledge of the Holy. HarperCollins Publishers, New York, NY, 1961.

About the Author

Staci L. Kitchen is a woman of God's wisdom and purpose. She is passionate about seeing the Body of Christ have an intimate relationship with God. She desires to release God's heart and wisdom in the earth through teaching, writing, praying, and equipping others to do the same.

Staci is a scribe, creative, and intercessor. She has a Bachelor of Science in Criminology and Criminal Justice and is currently working toward her Master of Theological Studies Degree.

She has been married for 27 years to Paul, has four children, a daughter-in-law, and two grandchildren.

www.ingramcontent.com/pod-product-compliance
Lightning Source LLC
Chambersburg PA
CBHW071514120626
46550CB00006B/2218